Who Wants to Be a Country Music Star?

The Right Way-The Wrong Way, and the Nashville Way to Launch and Maintain a Music Career!

by

Sam Wellington

authorHOUSE™

1663 LIBERTY DRIVE, SUITE 200
BLOOMINGTON, INDIANA 47403
(800) 839-8640
WWW.AUTHORHOUSE.COM

First published by AuthorHouse 04/21/05

ISBN: 1-4208-0578-9 (sc)
ISBN: 1-4208-0579-7(dj)

Library of Congress Control Number: 2004098724

Printed in the United States of America
Bloomington, Indiana

This book is printed on acid-free paper.

DEDICATION

A close friend of mine is not very optimistic about my attempt to become an award-winning author. In fact, he predicts this particular work will come out of the chute in paperback… as a COMIC BOOK. Hey, I'll take whatever writing success I can get. (Do you hear me, former close friend?)

Seriously, I would like to dedicate this writing effort to my wife Robin and our four daughters – Lisa, Shannon, Amy and Erica – who have shared most of the tears with me (happy and sad) through the years. Their support and tolerance of my career can never be measured or fully appreciated.

I would also like to acknowledge my Music Business mentors and friends – Jack Johnson and the late Dick Blake. I learned so much from these guys, including the art of knowing when to hold'em and knowing when to fold'em. Dick was responsible for helping to guide the careers of many Country Music Artists, including The Statler Brothers and Barbara Mandrell. Jack launched and guided the long-running careers of Charley Pride and Ronnie Milsap. At first, Dick was Jack's mentor (according to Dick). He used to say (affectionately – I think), "not so long ago Johnson would call me every morning asking advice on one thing or another. Now that Pride's a superstar, he calls me every morning giving me advice about everything."

I want to say thanks to Dave Barton, who for most of my professional career was my agent, business partner and friend – not always in that order. Raised near Sarasota, Florida and the headquarters of the Ringling Brothers Circus, I call Dave "THE GREAT BARTOONI." Had he ever joined the circus, he would have

v

easily become a star gymnast. I personally saw him walk into a Reno casino late one night – with drink in hand – and tumble down a flight of stairs WITHOUT EVER SPILLING A DROP!

Finally, I'd like to salute all my singing partners during those never to be forgotten 32 years, two months and six days on The Grand Ole Opry. They include the original members of The Four Guys vocal group – Brent Burkett, Richard Garratt, the late Berl Lyons and longtime group members Gary Buck, Laddie Cain, Glen Bates and John Frost. Other contributors include: Dave Rowland, Dan Stephens and Gary Judkins.

These super guys and super singers allowed me to share spotlights and stages around the world and help bring a little joy (I hope) to a whole lot of people. They further allowed me to stand on their shoulders and reach for the stars.

How many people who have had any degree of success can truthfully say they've never worked a day in their lives? I CAN – for 32-plus years, anyway! My longtime friend Jack Johnson (referred to earlier) has a totally different twist on the matter. Someone once called him a LUCKY S.O.B. Jack replied, "YEH, I AM A LUCKY S.O.B., and THE HARDER I WORK, THE LUCKIER I GET!"

Table of Contents

INTRODUCTION

Dear Readers...My name is Sam Wellington and I've just recently retired as a 32-year member of the World-Famous Grand Ole Opry in Nashville, Tennessee. During those many years on "The Opry" and on the Country Music Circuit performing with my group, *The Fabulous Four Guys*, ("fabulous" was a descriptive adjective that Hall of Fame DJ Charlie Douglas tagged onto our name), I've had a marvelous opportunity to see first-hand the countless changes in "America's Music" – both good and bad.

Prior to 1967, when I joined The Opry, Country Music had for the previous several decades, maintained a consistent identity and sound. However, by hosting network TV shows in the early, middle and late '60's, artists such as Jimmy Dean, Eddie Arnold, Glen Campbell and Johnny Cash took Country to an international level and brought millions of new fans to Country Radio; subsequently to the Country sections of record stores everywhere.

Most of these new fans were unable to fully appreciate the rural roots of the artists singing the songs, the songwriters who wrote them, the musicians who played them and the record producers who put each production together. Therefore, although those new fans liked what they were now hearing, they yearned for a touch of their former musical love – Rock 'N' Roll – and songs with a more uptown message to which they could better relate. These new fans were also younger and found it hard to connect with the much older recording stars who had dominated Country Music popularity charts for many years.

1

Record Companies, seeking to accommodate this newly found and younger record buying demographic, gradually set out to provide records with a stronger beat and place more emphasis on Rock 'N' Roll-style guitar players. At the same time, traditional Country musical instruments, such as the steel guitar and twin fiddles, were used much less often. Drastic change was imminent.

In the early '80s, Texan George Strait almost single handedly led a revolution – whether by design or by accident – for Country Music to return to its roots. He was joined by then newcomers Randy Travis and Ricky Van Shelton and later by Patty Loveless, Vince Gill, Alan Jackson, The Judds, Clint Black, Dwight Yoakam and eventual superstar Garth Brooks.

Through the years and through its many changes, Country Music today is alive and well. Yes, the artists are younger. No, the older Country acts are not heard much on the radio. But the music itself seems to have survived. The lyrics are stronger and more meaningful. The melodies are much more complicated and the performers are truly in a league of their own.

The information contained on the pages that follow is not meant to be construed as an exact blueprint to success in the Music Business, but rather a roadmap to help guide a novice in some of the right directions. In other words, no one can tell you exactly what to do to achieve that Super Platinum Album, but some of us who have been in and around "the big-time" for more than three decades can damn sure tell you what NOT to do!

Meanwhile, we hope those of you who have NO intention of taking a shot at success in the music field will still find this work, at the very least, an *"Entertainingly Good Read."*

SOMETHING ABOUT
THE AUTHOR

You might ask yourself, "WHAT'S A GUY LIKE ME, WHOSE NEVER HAD A BIG HIT RECORD, DOING WRITING A BOOK ABOUT HOW TO SUCCEED IN THE COUNTRY MUSIC CAPITOL OF THE WORLD, NASHVILLE, TENNESSEE?"

Well, I have pulled off a trick far more difficult than achieving Hit Record Status. I have not only survived but *prospered* in this "records only" city for more than 30-years, with music being my primary involvement. If enough of you buy this book, the length of my music tenure will most certainly be extended.

In order for the following work to have any credibility, I feel the need to provide you with some biographical background information on my NOT SO illustrious past. First off, I'm proud to say I am a former high school student, graduating 92nd in a class of 96 from Toronto High School in Toronto, Ohio. Cousins John Romey, the late Mike Romey, and Howard Nease finished below me. But hey, whada ya want? John and I were busy trying to get girls by singing in a "hot" high school group called "The Jets." Mike and Howard were busy trying to get girls by playing sports. John and I also played sports. He excelled at football and baseball, while I merely dabbled (or should I say dribbled?) in basketball. Studies just didn't seem all that important in those days. I'm sure I would have been far more embarrassed at graduation had I known we were accepting our diplomas in the order of our class rank. I thought I was nearly last because my last name began with "W."

Anyway, The Jets won a bunch of local amateur shows and nearly beat out a college folk group called "The Brothers IV" for a Columbia Records recording contract in New York City. The Brothers went onto great recording success while my Show Biz Career came to a sudden halt. I decided it was time to get serious about life. I joined the United States Navy, where I quickly learned that chipping paint aboard a ship was not what I wanted to do for a living. After my service stint, I proceeded to embark on a college career path while I worked as a beat reporter for a nearby small-town newspaper, The Steubenville Hearld Star (way to go Wellington…get a writing job first, *then* go to college and learn to write).

With an action-packed life now taking shape, I could see that "big bucks" were just around the corner, and the $65 a week I had been earning was soon to be little more than a laughing matter.

The following timeline is how my professional life began to unfold:

- Small-town newspaper reporter ($65 per week)
- Small-town radio continuity/news writer ($60 per week… wait a minute, I'm going backwards)
- Small-town radio newsman (five raises first year to $100 per week… ah, that's better)
- Small-town radio News Director (finally able to eat red meat on a regular basis)
- Small-town radio Operations Director
- Small-town radio Station Manager (all this by age 25… a regular Broadcasting Whiz Kid)
- Chucked it all for a singing career in Nashville, Tennessee, with a vocal group called The Four Guys (you gotta be kidding me - a group called *The Four Guys?*)
- Became big-time radio performer with regular cast member status on WSM'S *Grand Ole Opry*
- Became big-time touring pro with Hank Williams Jr., Charley Pride, Jimmy Dean, Marty Robbins, Ferlin Husky and Faron Young (one of the things I truly hate about show business is the constant name-dropping. Garth, Vince, Alan, The Chicks, and I were talking about this very thing just the other day)

4

- Became big-time TV performer on shows hosted by Bob Hope, Dinah Shore, Merv Griffin, Willie Nelson and Dolly Parton (strictly network - no more syndication for me)
- Became Small-Time Movie Star (sang one song in a Marty Robbins movie with my face barely visible and sang vocal backup for Webb Pierce in a mediocre Goldie Hawn movie called *Sugarland Express*)
- Became big-time night club performer in Las Vegas, Reno and Lake Tahoe, Nevada (got so good at club work decided it was time to buy one, so...)
- Became big-time night club owner/operator of The Four Guy's Harmony House in Nashville (we sang and ate prime rib for 10-years then quit while we were behind)
- During the next ten years, The Four Guys became The Beatles at sea (not literally – just very popular) with 75 weeklong cruises out of Miami and Tampa, Florida (swore for a time I was back in the Navy, but the money was definitely better)

So much for establishing my credibility. Let me now address my less-than-perfect writing style for a moment. Experts in the field say that I write with an alter-ego (I call him HOSS NOBODY). He is a separate personality that refuses to let me get too serious about myself and the words going into any piece that I prepare. For instance, just about the time I think I've written an award-winning sentence, HOSS will keep the computer keys moving with a follow-up line or comment in order to bring a certain degree of honesty to an oftentimes exaggerated statement. These afterthoughts, if you will, usually appear in parenthesis. My other self, HOSS, is a pain in the butt sometimes. However, because he is basically a "good ole' boy," I let him continue to write with me. I hope he doesn't disturb your reading flow too badly in the chapters ahead.

Aside from taking a rather humorous view of my life in the Entertainment Field, I have a very serious outlook toward this most challenging profession, A.K.A. "The Music Business." Over the years, I have often asked myself why someone hasn't written a truly informative book spelling out the basic do's and don'ts for a path to success in the world of music – a series of guidelines to help save a lot of young (and old) performers tremendous heartache and frustration.

Of course, there is no such thing as a guaranteed formula for success in any business, but there are a set of basic rules you must learn and a definite framework of thought you must acquire if you are ever going to "GET YOUR CHANCE."

Unfortunately, it usually takes many years (most times never) to find the correct signposts leading you to your personal pot o' gold. The music industry is probably the most difficult profession in which to find even the smallest degree of success. What's more, the hard knocks and frustration endured during the so-called "hungry years" are usually so extreme that it hardly makes the achievement worthwhile when and if it is ever attained.

Many young entertainers moving to Nashville are quick to cite the comparative rapid rise of some big names that came before them. But for every one of those you can name, there are literally thousands that fall by the wayside each year. Moreover, most of those so-called "fast rising stars" had to pay more dues than is generally known and most spent varying amounts of time held captive in this musical time warp called Music City, USA; held captive to await the final verdict of a supreme court made up of music insiders who may or may not ever acknowledge that a case was being presented for a hearing. A couple of writer buddies of mine – Randy Ahart and Rory Waters – wrote a song recently that sums up what I have just said. With the permission of their publishers – Jimmy and Melody Miles and their company, Rope 'n String Music – I am including the lyrics to a song called *THE NASHVILLE SCENE*:

> *"They roll into town everyday with the last dime that they own*
> *Some came to sing and some came to play and some are here to write a song,*
> *They come from every walk of life from California to Maine*
> *Just to be a part of the Nashville Scene...*
> *They packed their cars, and said goodbye to friends and family back home,*
> *And now the only chance they get to visit is on the telephone,*

They work in factories and tourist stores and sing for tips out on
the street,
Any way to survive in the Nashville Scene...

Chorus:

Some have hopes of singing on a stage
Or playing in a big-time studio,
Some dream about the day they see a banner hangin'
For a song they wrote down on Music Row,
Some will make it, MOST will fail
Some never will concede
But that's just a way of life in the Nashville Scene

Some will leave on a silver eagle with their name painted on the side
And some will go with nothing more to show than the satisfaction
that they tried,
Some have gone that couldn't stay for reasons unexplained,
And left their dream to die in the Nashville Scene!"

There is a beautiful melody that goes along with these true-to-life lyrics. This song has never been recorded commercially. One of the writers, Rory Waters, chalked up his first big chart-topper a while back as a co-writer on the *TRICK PONY* break-out hit, *POUR ME*. So now it's just a matter of time (in my opinion) before *THE NASHVILLE SCENE* and numerous other Rory Waters musical compositions find their way to the top of the charts.

Meanwhile, knowing only too well how difficult it is to climb the star ladder in Nashville, longtime Grand Ole Opry legend, the late Roy Acuff, had a humorous observation regarding the long road to music success. Crowned "The King of Country Music" many years ago, Mr. Acuff once mused that the normal Country Celebrity works an average of ten-years to gain their star status. Then once that status is achieved, the first thing they do is go out and buy a pair of sunglasses to hide behind.

As was stated earlier, sometimes it makes one wonder if the climb to fame and fortune is really worth the sacrifice it takes to get there. Once on top, the real work begins. Learning to deal with all the attention, peer pressure, lack of privacy, business and career decisions is certainly a full enough plate. But when you add the tremendous effects on ones family life, a real challenge suddenly emerges. Guess what folks, from the top there is no place to go but DOWN!

With that very cold, discouraging fact in mind, let's get on with the first of 35-chapters detailing the long road to "Show-Biz / Country Music Success."

CHAPTER ONE
YOU CAN'T WIN IF
YOU DON'T GET IN

Unfortunately, there is no college or university you can attend to learn the art of – and earn a degree in – the area of recording sure-fire hit records. With regard to most "normal" professions, you can go to school, study hard, learn a vocation, get a degree, plunge headlong into the working world with a good starting wage, and find yourself reasonable success in life. However, if your goal in life is to become the next KING or QUEEN of Country Music, there is a whole different set of rules to learn and a unique formula for reaching your goal(s). These rules and the formula can only be learned through experience; yours or someone else's. If you eventually learn your craft through your experiences, the path generally is long and winding. If you learn through the eyes of someone who has already been there, the path is still winding, but perhaps not quite so long.

The plan here is to pass along many of my experiences, good and bad, so that your road has white lines on both sides and one in the center, thereby making that road much easier to see and travel upon. The hope is also to avoid as many WRONG turns as possible.

The very first question you should ask yourself and others is *Do I have anything to offer the Music Business*? That is to say, do you actually have enough talent (real talent – not imagined or proclaimed by family and friends), and do you have enough drive and determination to stay the course and play in the "big leagues" of music? Confidence is one thing; blind faith and wishful thinking are something else entirely.

One way to find out if you actually have a special talent for singing and entertaining is to get out in front of people. Start performing at every local function you can, including talent shows, civic club programs, charities, benefits and any special event sponsored by your areas' Country Music Radio Stations. Let's establish something of major importance right here: if you plan to become the next Hank or Kitty, Porter or Dolly, George or Tammy or Garth or Trisha (it was by accident that I coupled the last two), you need to brand these words in your mind for now and evermore: ORGANIZATION, PROMOTION, RADIO and DISK JOCKEY.

Eventually, it takes an ORGANIZATION of people who strongly believe in you and are willing to offer some financial backing. A well connected Personal Manager is a good place to start. Entertainment Lawyers have just about taken over this role. There are very few up and coming managers who are not Attorneys (no more Col. Tom Parkers standing in the wings waiting to discover you or the next Elvis Presley). Your organization will eventually grow (if you ever get off the launch pad) to include an Attorney, Publicist, CPA, Backup Musicians, Bus Driver(s), Roadies, a Tour Manager, Concessionaire, and if you get big enough, a Hair Stylist and Makeup Person.

Your next step is PROMOTION. Through the efforts of your connected Personal Manager, you will need a Major Label Record Deal. Why a major label? Because the bigger the guns, the louder the shot. Major labels have the ways and means to promote the recorded product they release WORLDWIDE.

Your manager (and you) will still have to stay on top of things at your record company to be sure they live up to everything in your contract as it pertains to promoting your records and subsequently your career. Major Labels have the means to promote you in ways others can only dream about, such as "big-time" TV, Radio, Movie, and Sporting Events, as well as International Tours. Your own Publicist, working in concert with your Record Label and Talent Agency, can produce the results you'll need to stay on top as long as possible (you must realize now that when and if you do *MAKE IT*, you will not be King or Queen of the hill forever).

Let's talk about the last two components in this condensed equation – RADIO and DISK JOCKEY. D.J.'s can either be your best friend or your worst enemy. As an aspiring artist, here is the saddest commentary of all: your D.J. relationship(s) will always be one-sided, in that Disk Jockeys do not necessarily need you, but you don't stand a chance without them. Because of the introduction of Satellite Radio, the big-name personality local and/or regional D.J. is not quite as important as in days gone by. This is good news for the up-and-comer. Once upon a time, D.J.'s such as Ralph Emery, Bill Mack, Mike Hoyer, Lee Arnold, Larry Scott, Billy Parker, Charlie Douglas and others could have a large impact on an artist's career. Why? Because they hosted Country Music Shows on 50-thousand watt powerhouse radio stations and collectively could reach most of the population in North America. So, maybe D.J.'s such as those mentioned are not quite as necessary as before, but nevertheless they (those still active) or their stations are still influential. It's a good idea to accumulate a list of D.J.'s you meet and stay in touch with them (many will move from station to station). Keep them abreast of all your activities through phone calls, e-mails, birthday cards, holiday greetings and the like. I recently saw a bumper sticker that every recording artist should have Gold-Plated. It read, "TO GET IN THE GROOVE, LOVE A DISK JOCKEY." We should add *and SATELLITE PROGRAMMER.*

Do you write songs (not poems) or play a musical instrument? Both are considered big pluses in fostering a successful career in the Music Business. The more attractive you become as a commodity, the easier you will be to market. *Wait a minute*, you say. *What are we talking about? Creating an attractive cereal package at the supermarket?* Well, not exactly, but the analogy is remarkably close. Marketing is a keyword here. Perception oftentimes does become reality. With all the different cereal boxes on the grocer's shelves, what can be done to make one stand out more than all the others? Remember, talent and good looks alone very rarely win out (Alan Jackson, George Strait, and Allison Krause being just three exceptions). You must have talent – and loads of it. But you must also have, or acquire, as many other positive saleable attributes as possible, including *"Showmanship."* You see, the mission is to make yourself as attractive as you can in order to gain the attention of those in Music Power, and eventually to gain the attention of the record buying public.

If you do manage to catch the interest of a powerful Manager, Talent Agent or Recording Executive, he or she needs to have all the tools necessary to bring YOU to the forefront. Sometimes referred to as "flesh peddlers," Talent Agents or Managers look for every positive quality they can find in an act to determine whether or not that act has what it takes to hit the homerun ball and reach the top of the industry. As mentioned earlier, it takes loads of talent to make it in the Music Business, but personal appearance and overall image are key ingredients as well. Hairstyle, clothes, mannerisms, personality and weight are extremely important to those who want to create and market a particular image. Remember, *"Thin is always in." "Fat is never where it's at."* Though the day of the handsome Hollywood star look has passed somewhat, good looks and great physical appearance are still very important when it comes to "marketing" a performer (there's that word again).

The level of competition has risen drastically in the music industry during the past several years. Thousands of young, good looking, talented entertainers are vying for just a very few slots on recording company rosters. Even fewer slots are to be had on the nation's popular record charts.

So, to stand out in the crowd, one needs to think in terms of all those shelves at the supermarket and the thousands of items thereon. An aspiring artist needs to once again ask himself/herself, "what can I do to make my product (me) stand out over all the others on any given shelf?" Packaging is paramount. Then, you must deliver quality ingredients to back up the colorful exterior. This hopefully will lead to a satisfied music consumer. Even then, there are still no guarantees (tough business, huh?).

Perhaps I'm getting a little ahead of myself. Once you've exhibited your talents on a local level for a considerable length of time and have received what you consider to be good, honest reviews from those in your area, you should plan an exploratory trip to Music City, USA – Nashville, Tennessee.

It's possible that a long weekend or a week's vacation to Nashville will give you a glimpse first-hand of what the surface of the Country Music World is all about. Take a tour. Visit the homes of the stars, the recording studios, publishing companies and above all, visit the Country Music Hall of Fame and The Grand Ole Opry. All this to familiarize yourself with as many aspects of the Music Business as possible and thereby help prepare you for one of the biggest decisions you'll ever make...SHOULD I TRY IT OR NOT? Remember, information is knowledge and knowledge is power. The more knowledge you have, the better your chances are for success. I would suggest you subscribe to every Country Music Magazine your budget will allow. Watch all Country TV Shows available in your area. Learn what the top names already know about music styles, trends, clothing and imagery. Remember, these people are where you want to be. Put them under a microscope and stockpile the information you find there.

During my long career, I have been asked many times whether or not a certain individual should take a shot at a music career. For the longest time, I would respond with, "ONLY YOU CAN MAKE THAT DECISION." After seeing so many people over the years who never tried and regretted it their whole lives, I eventually began answering with, "YOU CAN'T WIN IF YOU DON'T GET IN." Better to have tried and failed than to have never tried at all. I sincerely believe that. One thing more though...don't wait to long to make your decision. The Nashville Music Business is shopping for youth AND YOU "AIN'T" GETTING ANY YOUNGER.

CHAPTER TWO
FINDING THE STARTING GATE
or
WHAT DO I DO FIRST?

After your exploratory trip to Music City, it's time to play 20-questions with yourself. Ask yourself the following:

1. What is my financial picture? (do I have the necessary staying power?)
2. How determined am I to *make it?*
3. How much patience do I have?
4. How much family support is there?
5. Is my wife/girlfriend/husband/boyfriend the jealous type?
6. How well do I deal with the public?
7. Do I have a drug or alcohol problem?
8. Do I write songs and if so, are they any good?
9. How punctual am I (late for meetings, etc)?
10. Do I have a college or armed services background (those who have lived away from home tend to be more disciplined and more mature)?
11. Do I pay my bills on time and take care of personal affairs (remember: the other half of Show Business is BUSINESS)?
12. Can I take direction and am I manageable?
13. How well will I handle working the road and living away from home?

14. Do I understand promotion/marketing and the need to do FREEBYS in order to advance my career?
15. Am I capable of accepting constructive criticism and unsolicited advice?
16. Do I understand the need for a slim, youthful and current image?
17. Why do I want to be a success in music?
18. Am I seeking only FAME and FORTUNE?
19. Am I simply on an *ego trip*?
20. Or, do I just have a God-given talent that I want to share with the world (if you answered *YES* to #20, don't ever let anyone talk you into taking a polygraph examination for any reason)?

Once you've answered these 20 questions to your satisfaction and to the satisfaction of those family and friends around you, and assuming you think you've got what it takes to get in the game, start getting your ducks in a row. That is to say, start saving money, honing your skills in every area previously mentioned and set a tentative target date to make your move to the bottom rung of the entertainment ladder.

Make sure you have adequate transportation (a car that's paid for), plenty of clothes that fit the image you've decided to start out with (your homegrown image will probably change when you connect with those in the know, but you need to start somewhere) and enough money saved to last a few months without working. However, finding a part-time job immediately will serve you well. Try to find something where you might come into contact with people in the Music Business and near the heart of the industry called "Music Row." Suggestions include, becoming a Hotel Valet Driver, Limousine Driver, Bartender or Waiter. Remember, Kris Kristofferson was once a janitor at Columbia (Sony) Records, and Alan Jackson once worked in the mailroom at the now defunct Nashville Network. John Anderson was a roofer who worked on the construction of the new Grand Ole Opry House back in the '70's. The important thing is to keep the pressure off yourself in the areas of wondering where your next meal is coming from and whether or not you will be able to keep a dry roof over your head.

When our group (The Four Guys) moved to Nashville, we had a Personal Manager who was dead set against us finding work to support ourselves while we pursued our careers. His philosophy was that if you worked at a regular job, the music industry will think you're not successful. Well, listen up buddy. We WERE NOT successful and nearly starved to death while we figured out what to do. He was right in many other ways, but totally wrong in this regard. My advice? DON'T BE ASHAMED OR TO PROUD TO GET A JOB!

Speaking of keeping a roof over your head, there are lots of inexpensive efficiency apartments in and around Music Row. This is where you need to relocate. Also, music insiders congregate in various little coffee shops, restaurants and bars in the Music Row Area. Find these local hangouts, and begin having coffee or lunch there too.

Your best source of inside information will come from others like yourself who are trying to get started. You'll find your new soon-to-be circle of friends at local music haunts around town. Tootsie's Orchid Lounge, Robert's Western World, Legends Corner and Wolfy's Honky Tonk on lower Broadway, Broken Spoke and Gabe's Lounge near Trinity Lane and The Nashville Palace across from The Opryland Hotel are just some of the most popular at the time of this writing.

There are many other showcase rooms, such as The Station Inn, Douglas Corner, Third and Lindsay, Twelfth and Porter, and the nationally known Bluebird Café in the Green Hills section of the city, to name a few. Still other clubs are being developed and coming into prominence in a former tourist area very close to Music Row. THE TIN ROOF currently leads this group in popularity.

Randy Travis, Terri Clark, Ricky Van Shelton, Gretchen Wilson and BR-549 are but a few of the many Country acts who got their starts in local clubs such as those mentioned. As soon as you hit town, get yourself to one of these or other similar local watering holes where you can get up and show your wares. Introduce yourself and turn on the charm. Don't be phony. Be yourself. But always be pleasant. Be funny. But don't be a smart ass (do you know why they don't send mules to college? 'cause nobody likes a smart ass).

Don't be a gossip and try to always have something nice to say about everybody. MAKE FRIENDS. Nashville is unlike any other entertainment town I've ever seen. People here do things for their friends. You'll find many helping hands if you're liked.

Meanwhile, when it's time for you to get up in front of your new club crowd and perform, try to select a Country Music Golden Oldie (up tempo) to start with. You'll probably only get to sing two songs your first time on stage, so after your opener, thank the back-up band, the host and the audience. Have something clever prepared to say and introduce your next song. If you are a writer, do your best original work. It's never too soon to begin losing the image of being just another "cover act." That is to say, original material (yours or someone else's) is what's going to eventually get the attention of a music insider. That said, in order to work clubs for pay, you'll need to learn as many hit country songs - past and present - as humanly possible to use in your own shows. The general public does not like unfamiliar material. You can always squeeze in one or two originals during each 45-minute stage set, but more than that is a quick way NOT to get yourself a return booking.

Here are some final words of wisdom in this chapter: WANT TO BE A STAR? WANT TO BE A WINNER? LOOK LIKE ONE AND THINK LIKE ONE!!

CHAPTER THREE
PREPARING FOR
THE BIG BREAK

So you've acted on my suggestions thus far and decided you've got that "special something" to join the ranks of Nashville Country Music Wannabes. With an exploratory week's visit to Music City under your belt, what's next? It's time to start saving money in order to survive for several months. Pay off the car, decide on your first "homegrown" image, buy the clothes and groom yourself to fit that new image.

At this point, another shorter visit (maybe a long weekend) to Nashville might be in order to locate potential housing and to explore part-time job opportunities. Even though you'll be financially able to survive for a period of time, a job right from the get-go would really put you in the driver's seat for security purposes while you launch your career. Having a backup bank account or emergency fund while living off your earnings from a job is truly the way to go.

Let's assume you've made your move, gotten an apartment and part-time job and are beginning to make your nightly rounds of music "hot spots." One of the best stops you can make on your way to your first stage is a friendly facility just off Music Row – Local 257 of The Nashville Musician's Union. This is where the top (and bottom) musicians in the city congregate to pick up checks, drink coffee and swap music tales with each other. The A.F. of M.

(American Federation of Musicians) and AFTRA-SAG (American Federation of Radio and Television Artists and Screen Actors Guild) have played important roles in helping to build the entertainment industry nationally, specifically with regard to The Nashville Recording Business. So join both unions ASAP – the former first and the latter as soon after as your budget will allow. Both unions require one-time initiation fees of several hundred dollars each. Call for the latest information (A.F of M. 615- 244-9514 and AFTRA-SAG 615- 327-2944). Union offices are great sources for lots of necessary information, and both are willing to help newcomers. Initially, it's all about networking.

Next, you'll need some promotional tools to help you begin marketing yourself. You're all you've got at the moment so don't be shy. Among your new music crowd will be someone who knows someone who will inexpensively prepare a biography (bio) for you. Your credentials to date can't be too impressive, but a little history on yourself listing any interesting accomplishments and your burning desire to be successful in music would be useful. A hot photo session to produce current color/black and white promotional photos is a must. Along with 8 X 10 glossies, a montage of photos showing various sides of your personality can also help project you in many ways. Remember, a picture is worth a thousand words.

Any local printer will provide you with your MOST important promotional tool – business cards. The more clever you can be with your card preparation, the better (i.e. cool logo, etc.). Don't forget to list your current phone number and keep your cards updated should the numbers and addresses change.

Now that you have a bio, photographs and business cards, a trip to an office supply store will provide you with colorful or plain white press kit folders to house your new wares (don't leave home without press kits).

Remember I said friends do favors for their friends in Nashville? As soon as YOUR circle of friends permits, get some help in acquiring the missing link in your promotional package – A DEMONSTRATION or DEMO TAPE. There are many small studios all over town where you can record inexpensively. When circumstances permit, put together a Speculation – Demonstration

Session to record your best stuff. Among your new friends will certainly be a guitar player and probably a bass man, keyboard player and drummer. Chances are you'll have little trouble getting them to provide studio backing for your music with the promise that you'll help them with one of their future music projects. A couple of songs is all you need initially — one up-tempo and one ballad.

Use original material if possible, so long as it's really, really, really GOOD. You'll soon learn the difference between The Good, The Bad and The Ugly when it comes to original songs. Be sure to not only record good songs, but record songs which show your range and style as a singer. And by the way, it's not necessary to sing every vocal lick you ever learned on every song you sing. TASTE IS KING! Vocal gymnastics should enhance, not rule the material.

It's a good idea to place yourself in a recording studio every chance you get. Recording experience is what you need and demo recording (yours or someone else's) is a great way to gain valuable time in the studio. Also, as you gradually stockpile original recorded material that you own, you'll soon have enough to prepare your own CD, which can be sold on site at your club or special event engagements. You'll be surprised at the added revenue CD sales can bring to your coffers. Many acts starting out use these funds to finance additional recording ventures, update their promotional folders and in some cases PAY THE RENT!

While we're on the subject of income, earnings from the Music Business automatically create a new category in your taxable life. With your first earnings, you'll become an INDEPENDENT CONTRACTOR. That is to say that you'll be responsible for any monies you earn in the Music Business and owe Uncle Sam appropriate Income and Self-Employment (Social Security/FICA) Taxes at the end of each year. Chances are those taxes will be withheld by your employer at your part or full-time job, but you'll be held liable for any funds earned elsewhere. While you're visiting your local office supply store, pick up a tax book and start keeping good records. Keep every expense receipt and every pay stub related to your work in music. My/our (remember, I was in a group) first tax book was nothing more than a cheap ledger I bought at K-Mart (we didn't have Wal-Mart in those days). I created two columns:

HERE'S WHAT WE MADE and HERE'S WHAT WE PAID! In addition, it's important for you to hook up with a good Music Business accountant (and there are many) at the earliest possible time.

As we prepare for that first big break, let's talk about another new word soon to join your Music Business vocabulary – COMMISSIONS. Whether you're working with a Personal Manager or a Talent Agency, they will want their fees for services rendered paid in the form of commission. In other words, they will require a percentage of your earnings. Most Talent Agencies will charge anywhere from 10 to 20 percent for any booking they arrange. If you're working exclusively with an agency, the fee is charged for any engagement you work, whether they booked it or not. Sometimes your agency will split commissions or percentages with another agency arranging a performance date. They usually work that out by mutual agreement. You will pay your full commission to your agency and they will pay a second or third party involved. A HUGE point to remember here: PAY YOUR COMMISSIONS IN A TIMELY FASHION, preferably as soon as you play the engagement and return home with your earnings. One of the best ways to get off on the absolute WRONG FOOT is to not pay your agency commissions on time. It's also the best way to get passed over for future bookings.

Your Personal Manager should be treated the same as your Talent Agency, depending on the terms of your agreement. Some PM's get theirs off the top, especially those who control the acts' checkbook. Personal Manager's service fees will vary. Colonel Tom Parker is said to have charged Elvis Presley 50 percent and had a lifetime contract with him. One newer member of the Country Music Hall of Fame and one of Country Music's all-time biggest record sellers is said to have signed a similar contract, less the lifetime clause in lieu of a ten-year clause. Don't fall for such a deal in either case. A manager who is truly interested in a long-term career for you will offer you a contract which starts small and escalates as your career escalates.

Above all, you have to build in an exit strategy for yourself should your manager not be living up to the terms of your agreement. You don't have an unlimited number of years to waste. When it comes to settling on a Personal Manager, it's important for you to try to get it right the first time. It's good to have great feelings for your PM and to create what you hope will become a long-lasting relationship, but when you sign that contract, remember it's strictly business. Believe only what's in writing. No court in the land will rule in your favor for invisible items between the lines. In other words, make plans for the divorce before the marriage! This is a difficult task, but you have got to look out for YOURSELF always, especially in the beginning.

Here's an ugly thought to ponder: You expect your Personal Manager and Talent Agent to be true to their word in every action made on your behalf, so it's important that you be true to yours. Many PM's and TA's regard most entertainers as "whores," because many would lie, cheat and sell their next born to make it in the Music Business. A well-known and well-respected PM once said, "I don't understand it. I work my tail off for an act; they find their way out of our contract and go to WILLIAM MORRIS. If I DON'T work my tail off for an act, they STILL go to William Morris (William Morris is one of the top entertainment agencies in America)." The moral of the story: be fair, be honest and make your word your bond. That is to say, if you tell someone it's going to rain, don't be surprised when they run for their umbrella.

One of the top talent agencies in Music City for the past 35-plus years has been and continues to be Buddy Lee Attractions. Founded by one-time professional wrestler, the late Buddy Lee, to book and handle the career of Hank Williams, Jr., the agency is now run by a well-respected Talent Manager, Tony Conway, and Mr. Lee's children. When asked to contribute some of his thoughts for a Nashville Newcomer, Mr. Conway listed several insightful suggestions. Among them was the sage advice of "picking the brains" of as many people in the professional Music Business as you can get around without becoming a "pest."

I'll always remember the sarcastic words of my longtime friend BIG JACK BARLOW, who once told me "A FRIEND IN NEED IS A PEST." Or maybe it was comedian Joe E. Lewis who said that. Anyway, in most cases, that philosophy does not apply in Nashville. Oddly enough, there are many people in high places in this "music town" who (when they have time) are more than happy to pass along their insider's wisdom. The keywords are "when they have the time." By the way, never ask for help, ASK FOR ADVICE.

Meanwhile, Mr. Conway suggests you make a plan ASAP to talk to at least three representatives in each of the following areas: Personal and Business Managers, Talent (booking) Agents, Publicists, Record Executives, and Entertainment Attorneys. Get each of their takes on the Nashville Music Industry. This will give you a well- rounded snapshot of how you can better guide your career path.

CHAPTER FOUR
THE THIRD COAST –
YOUR NEW HOME

Along with being known as MUSIC CITY, USA, Nashville has also been tagged "The Third Coast," a label that groups it with the other two major entertainment capitals – New York and Los Angeles – which occupy the East and West coasts respectively. There is so much more to learn about Nashville than the information supplied by the local Chamber Of Commerce and/or the Tourism Department. Since you intend to take up residency and make this "music mecca" your new home, it's extremely valuable for you to know when, why and how Nashville was able to grow from a relatively small southern community to the giant music mill it is today.

I think most everyone here would agree that the initial seeds were sewn by the National Life and Accident Insurance Company and a gentleman by the name of George D. Hay, a broadcast personality on the company's 50-thousand watt clear channel radio station, WSM. Those broadcast call letters – WSM – represented the insurance company's slogan, "WE SHIELD MILLIONS." George Hay was known on the air as the "Solemn Ole' Judge."

One November evening in 1925, while trying to come up with a clever segue from a network show being aired called GRAND OPERA to a down-home, pickin' and grinnin' local show, Hay had no idea that what he was about to say would become historic. "And now," Hay said, "we go from Grand Opera to THE GRAND OLE OPRY. LET 'ER GO BOYS."

The show was originally called the WSM Barn Dance, but the name was officially changed to The Grand Ole Opry in late 1927. Those early years saw mostly musicians playing in string bands as the featured entertainers, including an African-American harmonica player named DeFord Bailey. More singing and less "pickin'" became the commercial sound when Roy Acuff and his Smokey Mountain Boys and Bill Monroe and his Bluegrass Boys joined the show cast in 1938 and 1939. Suddenly, the need for more entertaining acts became evident, and Cousin Minnie Pearl was added in 1940. A short while later Ernest Tubb joined this elite group of performers. Soon, Stringbean, Grandpa Jones, Red Foley, Hank Snow and Kitty Wells came aboard, followed by Little Jimmy Dickens, Eddie Arnold, The Louvin Brothers and others. The "All-Star" cast was rapidly forming.

All the while there were many other Country Music Shows and entertainers springing up around the nation. Shows such as: The WWVA JAMBOREE in Wheeling, WV; The WGN BARN DANCE in Chicago; The LOUISANA HAYRIDE in Shreveport, LA; and THE OZARK JUBILEE in Springfield, MO. However, Nashville became the hub for most and THE OPRY became the biggest and most respected of all.

Music publishing companies began to evolve in order to supply the many new artists with recording material. Then recording studios soon followed, along with major label recording companies. The new Nashville Music Industry began to see substantial growth in the late '40's and early '50's when it started to produce recording stars like Hank Williams, Eddie Arnold, Carl Smith, Don Gibson, Pat Boone, Elvis Presley, Brenda Lee, Webb Pierce, Faron Young, The Everly Brothers, Roy Orbison, Jim Reeves, The Browns, Sonny James, Patsy Cline, Don Gibson and Bobby Helms. Their recordings were not only topping the charts in Country Music but were crossing over to the Pop/Rock'N Roll fields and having huge success there as well.

Of the many new music producers one man stood out above them all. His name was Owen Bradley and he was largely responsible for creating the so-called "Nashville Sound." Mr. Bradley was a one-time orchestra leader whose creative abilities it seems were limitless. Along with producing numerous hits for many of the stars just mentioned – primarily Brenda Lee, Patsy Cline and Bobby Helms – he would later produce most of the big records by Loretta Lynn, Conway Twitty, Bill Anderson and just about everybody who recorded for Decca (later MCA) Records in the '50's and '60's.

The heart of the Nashville Sound was developed over time not only by talented record producers like Owen Bradley but with the help of some extremely creative session musicians, such as: Piano men Floyd Cramer, Bill Purcell, Hargus "Pig" Robbins and Jerry Smith; Guitar stylists Chet Atkins, Grady Martin and later Jerry Reed (yes, that Jerry Reed); Yakety-Sax Saxman Boots Randolph; Steel Guitar innovators Pete Drake and Lloyd Green; Drummers Buddy Harmon and Kenny Buttrey and Bass Guitarist Bob Moore provided the rock-solid foundation necessary for any musical group to properly gel. Vocal back-up session groups like The Anita Kerr Singers and The Jordanaires added their special musical touch to give Nashville a distinctive sound readily identified when heard on the radio. This special group of session musicians and singers came to be known as The Nashville "A" Team. Their ability to relax and create in the recording studio soon gave Nashville a laid-back reputation admired by music communities around the world, including the other two coasts. Suddenly, it seemed everyone wanted to record in Nashville. Even non-country acts like Bob Dylan, Ringo Star, Bobby Vinton, The Byrds, The Mills Brothers and many others were anxious to work with this new innovative group of Nashville music people. Those collaborations and subsequent hits they produced served to broaden the city's appeal both as a recording capital and as an international tourist destination.

Today, between six and eight-million tourists trek through this music town annually looking for a glimpse of their favorite recording star or checking out the countless sites where the Nashville Sound was created. You may want to call it Music City, USA, or by it's insider's label, The Third Coast. However, you may just want to call it YOUR NEW HOME.

CHAPTER FIVE
CHASING THE DREAM

One of the most talented and entertaining groups I have ever seen in Nashville was a bunch of guys from Indiana called THE WRIGHT BROTHERS. This group hit town in the middle '70's and seemed destined for super stardom. They – through the tireless efforts of their Personal Manager (and friend), Marv Dennis – acquired a major label record deal, chalked up some minor chart hits, all the while becoming the toast of the town at the city's top club venue, The Stagedoor Lounge in The Opryland Hotel. They also became regulars on the Nevada night club circuit and were in big demand for special events and convention engagements.

After more than ten years of moderate success, it seemed their BIG BREAK was about to happen. Their manager introduced the group to an old Army buddy, Garry Marshall, producer of the *HAPPY DAYS* TV Show and countless other TV and Film successes. Marshall liked what he saw heard from "The Wrights" and asked them to compose all the music and perform it in an upcoming movie called *OVERBOARD* starring Goldie Hawn and Kurt Russell. Some ten songs were written and recorded for the movie. However, most of their music scenes ended up on the cutting room floor, and The Wright Brother's performance role was reduced to insignificance. The group became so discouraged they quit the Music Business and moved back to Indiana. Shortly thereafter, I ran into Marv Dennis at a local music function and asked him what had happened to the

Wright Brothers. He replied by saying the boys told him they were just tired of "CHASING THEIR DREAM."

The lesson here is that they gave it their all. They had considerable success but were not able to hit the "BIG-TIME." More than likely, it was through no fault of their own. Circumstances just did not allow it. Maybe they should have continued to try a little while longer. Maybe that "big hit" was just around the corner. But then, maybe it was just not in the cards no matter how long they stayed in the game. The important thing is for the individual group members to be contented with their time in the spotlight and with their decision to call it "quits" when they did.

This brings up the question, "HOW LONG SHOULD YOU CHASE YOUR DREAM?" Of course, only *you* can decide your timeline for music success or failure. Let me say here, there are lots of folks who couldn't quit no matter what. That is as it should be, especially those with something special to offer. Maybe you won't become the next Garth, Alan, Faith or Shania. But maybe you have found a special songwriting ability, or have become interested in producing, managing or booking. It's still the Music Business and if you love it, by all means don't leave it....EVER! Case in point, Jack Barlow (mentioned earlier). A former Indiana Disk Jockey, he came to Music City with a big, deep country voice and a 6'5" frame determined to make it as a recording star. He did, in fact, have a couple of hits in the early '70's and managed to get some of his own original material recorded by other artists. Here's a Country Music trivia question that stumps folks every time: the legendary pop group, The Mills Brothers, once had a big country hit called *CAB DRIVER*. Here's the question: who wrote the song they recorded for the "B" side of that 45 rpm hit? You guessed it - Big Jack Barlow. Though his recording career never blossomed as well as he had hoped, Jack ultimately made a small fortune doing hundreds of commercials. He represented many national sponsors on radio and television, most notably Big Red Chewing Gum. It was Jack's voice we heard for years singing the line, CHEW THE GUM CALLED BIG RED.

Someone once said, "success is a journey, not a destination." You be the judge of your own success and decide just how much of it you wish to enjoy. The late Roy Acuff, Minnie Pearl and Grandpa

Jones continued to perform throughout their '70's and enjoyed their success to the end. Legendary performers such as Willie Nelson, Porter Wagoner, Little Jimmy Dickens, Dolly Parton, Glen Campbell, Loretta Lynn and many others have never let age or waning popularity remove them from the stage or recording studio. However, if you are not fortunate enough to achieve a comfortable level of success in music – in any capacity – and "hanging in" simply means continued frustration and disappointment, by all means don't be afraid to "toss in the towel" and get on with your life. There IS life elsewhere. Start checking out the "second most important" thing you wanted to try when you were a kid. The dream is only worth chasing as long as you are happy chasing it.

CHAPTER SIX
POLITICS AND THE GOOD
OLE BOY MUSIC ROW CLIQUE

Up to this point, I have been very honest in my approach to this writing effort.Now, it's time to get BRUTALLY honest. Earlier, I said Nashville music people do things for their friends. Perhaps it has been a bit overdone by the "powers that be" on Music Row. So much so that many say there is a closed clique on "the row" that's nearly impossible to crack. I've heard this since moving to Music City in 1967. Believe me, there is no group or association here that can't be penetrated. For instance, anyone who was in music power in 1967 has all but retired to that great guitar-shaped home in the sky. The reins have been handed to an ongoing group of individuals who have managed to join the so-called clique over the years. Yes, there is and always has been a clique in the Music Industry. There is in *any* industry. But here, it's more than a clique. It's a small group of proven Producers, Writers, Publishers and Talent Managers who choose to work with each other because they know they are dealing with the best in their respective fields. But quite frequently, each record company, publishing house or talent agency WILL reach out and try a new, unproven talent and give them a chance. One thing for sure, the so-called "glass ceiling" for women has long since been penetrated in Nashville. The likes of Donna Hilley, who headed up the city's largest publishing company – *Tree Music* - and was later named head of Sony/ATV Music, along with the heads of the three major song licensing firms, AMERICAN SOCIETY OF COMPOSERS, AUTHORS and PUBLISHERS (ASCAP), BROADCAST MUSIC, INC. (BMI) and SOCIETY OF EUROPEAN STAGE, AUTHORS and COMPOSERS (SESAC) are now or have been run by women. So now we learn that the Good Ole' Boy Music Row Clique – to whatever degree it exists – just might (and I say might) include some Good Ole' *Girls* too.

Early on, I was told that in order to succeed in Nashville music, I/we would have to learn to talk Fishin', F…..' and Football. Because before any business was ever transacted, the "in-crowd" (an old term for clique) wanted to find out what type of person they were dealing with and enjoyed running a personality check on that person's down-home attitude. This made it doubly hard for a female artist to break into this seemingly macho circle. Many of the up and coming girl singers in years gone by were forced to become a little rough around the edges in order to appear like one of the boys while in their company. Many felt they had to go much farther in order to fit in (use your imagination).

The music row clique, whether real, imagined, partly real and/or partly imagined, is nothing that can't be dealt with in your career advancement process.

It's up to you to reach out and learn how to join the circle. Remember, you're on the outside trying to get in. The best approach is to develop (if you don't already have it) an out-going, pleasant personality and to become someone who is happy and "JUST SO PROUD TO BE HERE," to quote Minnie Pearl. Remember the old adage, "CATCH FLIES WITH HONEY, NOT VINEGAR." It's still in vogue today.

The Good Ole' Boy (and girl) syndrome is less prevalent these days, since many big corporations have consumed much of the local music community and have brought in executives with roots that are something less than rural. Because of this transformation, it's much more difficult to get next to music "big-wigs." However, when you do get an appointment or have an opportunity to participate in a business lunch, there is much more business discussed early on with a lot less small-talk beforehand. Again, let your well-connected Personal Manager decide when to talk fishin', whatever and football and at what point to cut to the chase, or as they say in the South, when to "fish or cut bait."

The thing to finally remember is that there have been very few *REBELS* who have made it big in Nashville. Don't use THE OUTLAWS as a success example. That was an image, not a real movement, though Waylon Jennings was a true rebel. If you try to do it entirely YOUR WAY, your Nashville venture will surely prove to be a painfully, frustrating experience, and more often than not, your road to success will grow longer and longer.

To offer you a true-to-life example, I once tried to help a young, talented country band go from playing music part-time to making an honest to goodness living in the full-time ranks. The group was made up of five better-than-average musicians, three average singers and one outstanding lead singer.

I arranged a showcase for the band at The Opryland Hotel, inviting everyone I knew in the Music Business to see and hear 45 minutes of their best stuff. Several music insiders were among the two-hundred or so in attendance. The boys were a smash hit with the crowd. One Talent Manager ran up to me and exclaimed, "Sam, before you die, you've got to will me that group." Almost unheard of, this band was off and running with only one showcase under their collective belt.

Immediately, they began earning top money in clubs both in the U.S. and Canada. I was able to arrange long-term contracts for them in the Cruise Ship Market for even better money. Now that they were eating regularly, it was time help them get to the next level – a major label recording contract. This task became much more difficult. After "turn-downs" by several labels, including RCA, Columbia and Atlantic (the lead singer *WAS* offered his own deal with Atlantic, but said no), it was arranged for the band to record with one of Nashville's leading studio engineers who had worked on many hit recording sessions, including numerous sessions with the group Alabama. He was also a great writer who recently chalked up CMA Song of the Year honors. At the time, he was trying to move up to producer level and needed a really good unknown act with which to work. Our Engineer-Producer-To-Be had plenty of big-time contacts with major labels and became excited about the opportunity to team up with the band I was helping. Everything was going well when suddenly, we had a large problem: the group members insisted that they play their own instruments on the sessions. Most artists use studio musicians on their recordings; musicians who are some of the best in the world and who are trained in the highly technical art of studio work. Our mild-mannered Producer strongly advised band members against playing their own instruments but said he would take them in anyway to see what they could develop.

Needless to say, the first session was a disaster. However, the Producer was still interested in the group, provided they lay down their instruments and use studio "pickers." They refused and the Producer promptly dropped out of the picture, only too emerge later with another new group who didn't care about playing instruments. The result created HITS for his new group called 4 RUNNER. Meanwhile, the band I had been working with fell by the wayside with their "my way or the highway" attitude. Just as my Producer friend had done, I decided to take "the highway" and get out of "their way" altogether.

In summary, politics and good ole' boys (and girls) make the world go around. It's not selling out to join in, listen and participate. It's called CAREER PROMOTION! Better yet, it's "good business."

CHAPTER SEVEN
REJECTION - LEARN TO
HANDLE IT OR LEAVE TOWN

While you're winning talent shows and becoming the "Toast of Your Hometown Area," you will find very few people ready to criticize your singing and stage work. In fact, you will grow to expect nothing but praise every time you step on stage. This is great in the beginning, since we all need a tremendous amount of encouragement to move from amateur status to that of becoming a true professional.

However, when you make the move to Nashville to officially launch your new music career, you will find things are a whole lot different. You will suddenly experience the wrath of critics at every turn; everyone from the owners of local nightspots where you first appear, to your new best friends (aspiring Music Business peers), who say they are merely trying to help you improve. "Constructive criticism" they call it, but criticism nonetheless. Immediately, you must develop a thick skin and learn to accept what sounds like good advice and discard the rest. Use common sense to make your determinations. If somebody tells you you're slumping at the microphone and chewing gum on stage, stand up straight and get rid of the gum. Chalk it off as a good critique; make the adjustment and improve.

Later, as you progress and begin doing stage shows (not dance sets) you'll find yourself being critiqued by media entertainment reporters. This is when you begin to find out whether or not you want to wear your feelings on your sleeves or learn to "suck it up," listen and move onward and upward.

For example, we (The Four Guys) were opening for Charley Pride on an International Tour with Cobo Hall in Detroit as our first major stop. A bit nervous, we charged the stage to do our high energy 25-minutes. We all were rather pleased with our performance and so was Charley. However, it seems the local newspaper critic wasn't nearly as pleased. In his column the next morning, he gave the show a good review overall but remarked that The Four Guys looked like four "Good Humor Men" dressed in solid white suits. After reading the article, Charley jokingly said, "well, at least he didn't say anything bad about your singing, and that's what really counts (but Charley, he didn't say anything good either)." HOSS, isn't it about time for your afternoon nap?

Opening for a Super Star at the peak of his career can be extremely rewarding yet oftentimes quite deflating. Occasionally, we would hear chants like, "WE WANT CHARLEY - WE WANT CHARLEY." One night in Chicago, we were in the middle of performing the one and only ballad in our opening set when the chants started. At the song's conclusion, I addressed the audience and said, "Ladies and Gentlemen, whether you believe it or not, Charley Pride knows we're out here. In fact, he's paying us to be out here. If you don't allow us to finish our opening act, he is really going to be upset with us. Do you want Charley to come out here upset and not do a great show for you?" Fifteen thousand people screamed "NO." We had no other problems the rest of the evening. This "SQUELCHER" as I called it became a regular part of our show whenever and wherever the chanters would appear.

It was opening night for the Charley Pride Show at the Hilton Hotel in Las Vegas. This was the hotel that Elvis ruled AND at the time he was ruling it. Needless to say, the engagement was very important to Charley, supporting act Ronnie Milsap and certainly the opening act, The Four Guys. It was the beginning of a long two-week stand at The Hilton, so early reviews in the Vegas newspapers were doubly important since they would impact show attendance for the entire run. As usual, the show got high overall marks, but the only act one reviewer picked on was "The Guys" when SHE said, "The Grand Ole Opry's Four Guys opened the show and performed 20-UNNECESSARY MINUTES." Talk about a blow to your ego. She didn't say we were good or bad but simply unnecessary. This was the same city where we had been dubbed "The Class Act of the Strip" by many critics only three years earlier. How quickly they forget.

These episodes of criticism were but a very few we received during our two and a half year tour with the Pride Show. Nevertheless, a bad review is never easy to swallow. It's how you deal with it that's important. Again, if its constructive criticism and you determine that it has merit, make the adjustment and grow from it.

Here's a petty thought - wouldn't it be nice to someday be in a position to critique some of the country's most vicious critics? You know, the ones who have a regular entertainment column to write and feel the need to blast every traveling and local act in town just to fill their allotted space and attract readership. Most critics I've encountered over the years have never performed on stage or ever sang a note outside the shower. Most wouldn't know a *FLAT NOTE* from a *SHARP ONE*. They have simply been around enough music people to pick up words like "PITCHY," meaning not singing consistently on pitch, in other words, slightly out of tune.

When it comes to critics, I'm reminded of the old joke where the Pope was addressing thousands in St. Peter's Square at The Vatican condemning the birth control pill. The Pope shouted, "NO MORE PILL - NO MORE PILL." A little Italian lady yelled back, "YOU NO PLAY-A THE GAME - YOU NO MAKE-A THE RULES."

That said, in my opinion, coverage of major college and professional sports have improved greatly since former players and coaches have moved into the broadcast booths, giving the boot to the know-it-all, I-NEVER-PLAYED-THE-GAME broadcaster.

Some Country Music critics have come to prominence through the use of sharp tongues and clever writing skills. Most, including at least two in Nashville, have a broad knowledge of Country Music history and can recite countless facts and figures from before The Carter Family and Jimmy Rogers to the present time. But what do they really know about the heart and soul of the Music Business, namely the songwriters and their very special talent; the performers and their ability to stylize a song and make it their own; and the producers who mold it all together in a recording studio and come up with hit music? Let's not forget the sales and marketing folks and the tireless efforts (and pressure) of the guys and gals who head up the recording companies and the three major music licensing firms who keep track of all the writer/publisher royalties.

If you think you can write, perform, create and market a hit song, I'll listen to you day and night as a critic. If you were raised in the country and grew up listening to Country Radio, you probably don't have to study facts, figures and offer amazing observations about a Country Music entertainer.

Chances are you'll have an idea what the lyrics of a country song and the singer singing it are all about the first time you hear it. Dolly Parton opened a network television show some years back with a song called, "IF IT'S COMIN' FROM THE HEART, IT'S FROM THE COUNTRY." So true, so true.

I've had only negative things to say about *SOME* critics — HOTDOGS who are out to make a name for themselves at the expense of hard-working music people. There is one reviewer who has the respect of everyone I know who has ever been the subject of his pen. His name is Joe Delaney. He has written for Las Vegas newspapers for more than forty-years that I know about. When he reviews a show you've participated in, you know it has been fairly judged from the opening stage lights and production to the performance and closings. As an entertainer, I know that a Joe Delaney critique is something to cut out, have framed and hang on the wall in your den or music room. Good or bad, you know it's fair. I think that's all that can ever be expected.

Every now and again, the public will confuse you as to whether or not your talent and presentation are truly appreciated. It's something like wrapping a compliment around a critique. Some would call it a "left-handed compliment."

I recall one specific occasion after a Four Guy's show in Knoxville, Tennessee. We had just completed a very successful performance, took our encore bows and walked to the side of the stage to meet, greet and sign autographs. Among those approaching the group was an elderly gentleman who asked me to sign his show program. While signing, he asked me if our group had ever performed at nearby University of Tennessee? I replied that we had never had the occasion. He then said, "you really ought to perform there sometime. They have groups over there all the time and a lot of them are WORSE than you guys." I thought a minute, then handed him his signed program and said, "THANKS, I THINK."

Just remember that rejection and criticism (not always constructive) are ever present factors in nearly every entertainment career. We all know what opinions are like, and everybody's got one. Just remember what the fella said when he kissed a mule, "EVERYBODY TO HIS OWN TASTE" (Sammy, I think the fella you speak of was JIMMY DEAN, and he wouldn't like you stealing his stage lines). HOSS, remember what the little Italian lady yelled to the Pope? I think the same phrase applies to most critics and to YOU!

CHAPTER EIGHT
THE NAME GAME

At some point early in your career beginnings, you should examine your name and consider its' future importance as it appears on a marquee or a CD. Some of us are lucky to have given names which will work no matter what profession we choose. Others, in fact most others, are given monikers, which are perfectly acceptable in any line of work EXCEPT in show business.

I remember my first day on the air as a News Broadcaster when a listener called in to find out what my *REAL NAME* was. She refused to believe that Sam Wellington was and is my real name. She simply said, "NO WAY," and hung up. Most of my colleagues in broadcasting had changed or shortened their names for listener appeal and simplification. We called them "stage names," "ten-cent names," etc.

If your name is ever to appear in lights, it should be one that people can easily remember, since one of the most difficult tasks in getting a career off the ground is acquiring name recognition. There should be something about your name that sticks in the public's collective mind, such as *SHANIA TWAIN*, rather than her birth name – Eileen Regina Edwards. If your name already has a good ring to it, don't ever consider changing it. What do I mean by a good ring? How about WAYLON JENNINGS, LORETTA LYNN, JOHNNY CASH, CHET ATKINS, PORTER WAGGONER, MERLE HAGGARD, BARBARA MANDRELL, MARY CHAPIN CARPENTER,

ALISON KRAUS, VINCE GILL, ALAN JACKSON and TOBY KEITH?

If you're trying to choose a name for a group, things get a little more difficult. The group ALABAMA was first called *WILD COUNTRY*, then *THE ALABAMA BAND*. However, it was feared they would be confused with the state's football team. As their popularity grew, the *BAND* part was dropped and they became simply, ALABAMA. DIAMOND RIO was originally formed as THE TENNESSEE RIVER BOYS and performed in one of the shows at Opryland USA Theme Park in Nashville. The name was changed when the group signed its' first major recording deal.

In the '80's and early '90's groups like EXILE, RESTLESS HEART, and THE KENTUCKY HEADHUNTERS brought an entirely new dimension to group names in Country Music, all but eradicating the more earthy, family and brotherly names; those such as: THE WILBURN BROTHERS, LOUVIN BROTHERS, STATLER BROTHERS, GLASER BROTHERS, GATLIN BROTHERS and THE BROWNS.

THE FOUR GUYS was a name spawned out of the '50's, when practically every group was named the four somethings or other, such as: THE FOUR FRESHMEN, THE FOUR ACES, FOUR LADS, FOUR COINS, FOUR SEASONS and FOUR PREPS, just to name a few. It was a name, bland as it is, that gained rapid acceptance by Country Music Fans but not by the music industry or even some group members, yours truly included. It was suggested numerous times that we change it. Names like *WINCHESTER, YOUNGER BROTHERS, THE 4 GOOD GUYS* were considered (notice the number "4" was substituted for the word FOUR). Roy Acuff used to introduce us by saying, "They came here (to The Opry) calling themselves The Four Guys. I didn't like that name so I gave them a better one. I call them MATTHEW, MARK, LUKE and CAIN and Cain is actually for real" (referring to our Tenor Singer, Laddie Cain). Finally, our D.J. Hall of Fame buddy Charlie Douglas began introducing us as THE *FABULOUS* FOUR GUYS. We decided to get comfortable with that and subsequently spent the next 20 years trying to live up to his added descriptive adjective.

A couple of eye-catching group names I have seen that really haven't caught on yet are *TENNESSEE PULLYBONE* and *DAMN SKIPPY*. I saw the name *SLICKERBILLY* on a trailer sign marquee in front of a local lounge and was so intrigued that I had to go inside to see and hear them. It turns out that two of the five band members were from Chicago (city slickers) while the other three were from the South (hillbillies) – hence, SLICKERBILLY. Some recording executives didn't care much for that name and talked the boys into changing it to *KINDRED SPIRIT* (Huh?). When their new name didn't advance their recording career the group changed it back to SLICKERBILLY, and they are certainly no worse off.

There are some oddball names (not given but chosen) that have been very successful through the years. Engelbert Humperdinck has certainly had a brilliant career, oddly enough recording "Pop" versions of country songs. The given name of ELVIS PRESLEY became a big hit the very first time most people heard it. However, given names like Leonard Sly and Bernie Schwartz probably would never have caught on in "Show Biz" circles, so it was a wise choice to change them to ROY ROGERS and TONY CURTIS respectively.

At the end of the day, if you think your given name is cool and will stand the test of time in the public eye don't mess with it. You know, "If it ain't broke, etc." On the other hand, if your given name is Roscoe Higginbothem, perhaps you might give a name change some consideration. However, a good case can always be made to keep or change a name, and compared to ENGLEBERT HUMPERDINCK, ROSCOE HIGGINBOTHEM is not all that bad!

CHAPTER NINE
CALLING ALL ENTERTAINERS!

When I came into Country Music there were mostly personality singers and very few entertainers. You know — ENTERTAINERS — guys or gals who go on stage with a plan to do more than just sing their latest single release or a cut from their last album. My career has been blessed with the opportunity to work with some of the best entertainers in the business, each contributing their individual specialties to greatly improve MY OWN stage performance (come on, Wellington...they didn't CONTRIBUTE their individual specialties, YOU STOLE THEM). HOSS, check the dictionary for the word "ANNOYING." Your picture is right next to it, or it certainly should be.

Later, I'll talk in some detail about a couple of these outstanding performers, but now I'd like to deal with your approach to show and stage work. The very first thing you need to understand is that an audience is made up of individuals who came to be entertained, not sung to sleep. Yes, if you currently have a hit record they certainly want to see (and hear) you sing it. If you've had a bunch of hits, they want to hear them as well. If you've had no hits, they'll want to hear (and see) you sing hits by other artists (new and old). Since we're assuming you have not made the "big-time" yet, let's deal with what your approach should be to YOUR STAGE and YOUR AUDIENCE.

I probably ought to tell you that the more successful you become, the faster an audience will accept your stage work. SUCCESS

BREEDS ACCEPTANCE. When an unknown comic tells a joke, it had better be very, very funny. On the other hand, Jay Leno or David Letterman can tell a mediocre story and get uproarious audience response.

So it's easier for a veteran performer to plan and execute his show than it is for a new kid on the block trying to get started. The best advice I can offer a newcomer is to make the crowd (assuming there is a crowd) like (or accept) you as soon after you hit the stage as possible. You ask, "how do I do that?" First off, charge the stage like you're thrilled to death to be there. Smile and immediately say something friendly. Get the audience involved in your presentation from the "git-go" (hand clapping, etc.). Use only cordless microphones so you're free to roam the stage left to right/right to left. Single out individuals in the audience; point to them and smile as though you're old friends. Keep your show moving with up-tempo material, using ballads only for pacing and effect. Remember – you have no hits, so you better be ready to deliver those of others in steady progression.

Pause briefly from time to time for some audience communication, but don't give them a chance to get bored or lose focus. It's up to you to hold their interest, so along with the hits of the day, integrate a few "blasts from the past" with some interesting dialogue about the original artists/writers who had first composed or performed the hits. Try to choose material with special meaning or to which your audience can best relate.

There has always been a special marriage between Country Music and Gospel Music, since most Country Stars got their start singing in church. Brad Paisley has said he was asked to sing in church when he was eight-years old; the congregation applauded and he was hooked. Anyway, a good ole' hand-clapping gospel song is a good fit in most Country Shows (clubs excluded).

A pitfall you most certainly will want to avoid on stage is pandering to or playing to your backup band. Yes, they (the band) will more often than not be kind and laugh at all your stories and cater to your every whim on stage, but you should never forget who or where your audience is. Bless the "boys in the band," but play to the crowd.

Tricks of the trade allow you to spice up your act during the course of your show with other things to do than sing and run around the stage. If you are talented enough to play more than one musical instrument, integrate a song or medley into your show displaying that talent. If you do impressions – particularly of other famous country entertainers – do a few. If there is a special tribute you would like to pay to a friend, family member or mentor, by all means pull up a stool, dim the lights to a pin-spot over your head and tell the story or sing your special song. Don't drag the moment out. Get to the point, say your prepared lines and/or sing your salute. Again, keep your audience focused on you and your message. As always, don't be afraid to show your pearly whites – don't hide them behind your microphone. Too many young performers feel the need to "eat the mike," thereby blocking the most effective portion of their face (their smile). Holding the mike a couple of inches below your mouth will allow it (and you) to do your respective jobs on stage.

Earlier, I said I would call out the work of at least two of the best entertainers I have ever seen. Through the years, I'm privileged to have worked with several, including: Faron Young, Ferlin Huskey, Marty Robbins, Barbara Mandrell, Hank Williams, Jr., and of course, Charley Pride. However, I must say that the absolute best entertainer I ever shared a stage with was Jimmy Dean. Everything good I ever learned about stage work I learned from "Ole' Big Ears" (his reference – not mine). It would take several chapters to do justice and adequately describe Jimmy Dean's approach to the stage and to show business. I'll simply try to sum up what I saw in him as he worked the crowd night after night. He always started them off laughing and then entertained them with a song or two. After that, he made them cry and laugh some more with true-to-life stories, and then he would bring them to their feet with a well orchestrated patriotic closing not a cheap patriotic shot. Finally, he would then take his encore – along with that pin-spot mentioned earlier – with a stool at center stage. Signifying that the show was drawing to a close, he would usually say, "WELL, AS THE FAT LADY SAID WHEN SHE TOOK OFF HER GIRDLE, THAT LETS ME OUT." Then, in a very quiet moment, he would begin to relate how thankful he was and how appreciative he was that he had been given the opportunity to be with this particular group of people on this particular night. He would tell of his humble beginnings, his rise to fame with records, including his monster hit *BIG BAD JOHN*, and his television success. He took no credit for himself, but rather expressed his thanks to the public and to all those who supported he and his family through the years. He would say, "YOU KEPT THE GROCERIES COMING INTO THE DEAN HOUSE WHEN WE NEEDED THEM SO BAD YOU CAN'T HARDLY BELIEVE."

He would close by saying, "AFTER THINKING ABOUT THIS ALL DAY TODAY, I JUST THOUGHT IT WAS ABOUT TIME I THANKED YOU." Then he would sing a verse and a chorus of YOU ARE MY SUNSHINE, MY ONLY SUNSHINE done as a ballad with only a piano accompaniment. The band would then join in, turning the song into a fast instrumental "play-off." Jimmy would take his bows; thank everyone on the show and say, "GOODNIGHT and GOD BLESS."

There was NOT a dry eye in the house as show after show, night after night (one engagement in Las Vegas ran two shows per night, seven nights per week for six straight weeks), the audience would leap to their feet with thunderous applause.

You might be saying would a Jimmy Dean approach work on a 21st century audience? That was then – this is now. Personally, I think much of Dean's stage act would be just as effective today as it was in the '60's, '70's and '80's. Some of his material would need to be updated of course, but his style and delivery would still be that at which most entertainers could and would marvel. I know I did – and still would.

The second performer whose work I greatly admire comes from today's cast of Country Music Stars. I first saw MARTINA MCBRIDE perform from my vantage point in the wings of the Grand Ole Opry Stage. It was her initial appearance. She sang like no artist I had heard since CONNIE SMITH burst onto the Country Music scene in the '60's. Coming out of such a small body, Martina's voice was so powerful. While I was amazed at her singing talent, I was not impressed with her stage presence. She merely stood there and sang. Good enough for a radio audience, but not good enough for those 4400-paid Opry patrons. Nevertheless, most of us who saw her first

Opry performance agreed that she would have a great career. Little did we know how great it would be.

I always enjoyed Martina's records on the radio but didn't pay much attention to her career overall until one afternoon aboard my boat in the summer of 2000. I was watching *The Willie Nelson Farm Aid Show* on The (now defunct) Nashville Network. Suddenly, Martina was introduced and she stormed the stage with the force of a Tennessee Tornado. She proceeded to perform 45-minutes of the greatest material (her hits) I had heard in years, closing with her signature hit –INDEPENDENCE DAY. She was stage left; she was stage right; she was center stage; she smiled and singled out various audience members as though she was performing at The McBride Family Reunion. She was serious; she was humorous; she was playful; but most of all she was *entertaining*. Such a drastic change from the shy little girl with the big voice I had seen during her first appearance on The Opry. I became a huge fan that day and now have a stack of her CD's to prove it (I bet you contacted her agent to get them FREE). HOSS, where would I be without your support? I'd like to find out someday!

Anyway, hit records remain the primary focus of any career, but selling them on stage with your own brand of salesmanship is important as well. Learn the tricks the pros know while adding a few of your own. Blend them all together and come up with your very own show presentation. Make one of your career goals to become one of the best at presenting yourself and your talent on stage. Enjoy yourself! Have fun! But most of all learn to become a GREAT ENTERTAINER!

CHAPTER TEN
HOLY CRAPOLA, BUBBA!
I GOT A RECORD DEAL!

I cannot believe it's finally happening. I've been in Nashville two-years, living in this tiny apartment, tending bar nights at Smokey Joe's Café and pitching my stuff to anyone who will listen. At long last, someone wants me to sign a long-term recording deal. So what that most people have never heard of BUCKSNORT RECORDS. Didn't you hear me? IT'S A RECORD DEAL! Where do I sign? Well cowboy, maybe we'd better talk this over for a spell before the big signing ceremony.

Let's find out a little something about Bucksnort Records. Let's see if they have a distribution deal with a major label or ANY distribution source (those deals *do* happen once in awhile). Next, let's check out their track record. Such as, what other acts are on their roster; how many national chart records have they had to date; what is the highest any of their recordings have ever charted and who are their producer(s)? What about their reputation and professional standing in the Nashville Music Community? And here's the biggest question: have they asked you to pay for the recording session(s), musicians, studio time, etc.?

Once you've done a little research into Bucksnort's history, chances are excellent that your so-called hot-off-the-press record deal needs to go bye-bye and you need to consider yourself extremely lucky that you had the common sense to think it through and decide against it. I'm not saying that recording for an independent label when you're just starting out is completely bad. Many older hit acts in Country Music got their start on small independents, like the group Alabama on MJD Records, Lynn Anderson on CHART Records, Sammi Smith on MEGA Records, Johnny Paycheck on LITTLE DARLIN Records, Vern Gosdin on BAKERSFIELD INTERNATIONAL Records, and George Jones on MUSICOR , just to name a few. In fact, independent record companies have (over the years) launched the careers of many recording stars. Signing with an independent company has often proven to be a great way to get noticed nationally with the eventual hope that a major label would step in and take over a proven product. The big boys would let the little guys take all the chances and make the initial investment. Then they (the major label) would make the small label an offer they couldn't refuse.

Trouble is, the artist would often face a huge royalty bill from their new *MAJOR LABEL*, as the artist is required to pay for all label expenditures made in their behalf through *future* royalties on record sales. Nevertheless, the artist would still be better off signing with a major label than hacking away with a small independent. Should hit records start happening, that royalty bill will eventually be reduced. Notice I said *reduced* and not *eliminated*. The label will never let you get out of their debt completely. They hold on to as much of your royalty earnings as they can for as long as they can. How do they do this? By continuing to record you, thereby further running up your tab.

Should your career get big enough and at some point you decide to challenge their bookkeeping practices (like The Dixie Chicks once did with Sony Music), you just might see some additional royalty payments. It takes a truly major act to go up against a powerful record company. Be sure you know exactly where you are on the label's food chain before you decide to try.

Meanwhile, back to YOUR Bucksnort Records deal. If you've kicked around Music City awhile without much success and the guys and/or gals at Bucksnort seem really interested in trying to produce a hit record on you, it might be beneficial to begin a little dialogue which could eventually lead to a record release. If the independent label is solid locally and they're willing to foot the bill, a one or two-record deal with options based on chart success might be worth the time and effort for them and you. No long term deals, though. Be sure you get mutual voice in the choice of material to be recorded and mutual voice regarding any product to be released to the public. In addition, be sure you have mutual say with their creative team on practically everything. Agree to a one-year deal (tops), granting a couple of option years if they come through with a Top 50 or higher record out of the chute for you. However, that's highly unlikely without a high-powered record promotion team working each of your releases. Unlikely yes, but not impossible.

The worst thing that can happen to you (if you signed a short-term contract) is that your career will be on hold for that period of time. The good news is that maybe you'll have a good enough record release (or releases) to get your name and talent out there on the radio air waves and start building yourself a grassroots fan base. Let me reiterate (listen Wellington, don't you first have to ITERATE before you *RE*-iterate?). O.K. HOSS, I'll do it your way. First I'll say that a small label deal should not be out of the question. However, it should be entered into with great caution and with a definite short-term exit strategy. NOW I'LL SAY IT AGAIN (reiterate) with fewer words. If you do it, BE CAUTIOUS!

CHAPTER ELEVEN
WHO NEEDS A FAN CLUB?

Before we even attempt to answer that question, anyone hoping to become successful in any phase of public life should realize that *FAN* is short for *FANATIC*! When you idolize someone to the point that some fans do, there's a good chance that fan is desperately lacking something major in his or her own existence. However, to really dig a person's music, acting ability or stage persona and to hold that person in high esteem with respect and admiration is (I believe) a perfectly natural occurrence.

We all like to have role models – people who set good examples for ourselves and our children. The problem with our world today is that we don't have enough positive role models. It was easy when I was growing up in the '50's and '60's. I remember my childhood heroes were Roy Rogers (King of The Cowboys), Gene Autry, John Wayne, Hopalong Cassidy, and my all-time favorite, Tex Ritter. Tex later became one of my heroes in adulthood and a very important mentor to me individually and to the Four Guys collectively. In fact, one of the hardest tasks of our professional career, yet one of the greatest honors we ever received, was to be invited, at his request, to sing at his funeral. I'll never forget that cold, blustery winter day in January 1974. I had just returned home from Ohio after spending the holidays with family. The prior 36-hours had been spent in a car stopped during a terrible ice storm just south of Elizabethtown, Kentucky. We hadn't heard the news that the great cowboy movie and Grand Ole Opry Star, Tex Ritter, had passed away. Just after arriving home in Nashville, the phone rang. It was Dorothy Ritter, Tex's wife. She gave me some details of his death and said he had specifically asked that his favorite group, The Four Guys, sing his favorite western song at his funeral. The song was called ROUNDED UP TO GLORY. None of us had ever heard the song previously, but we hurriedly got the group together and immediately headed to the church where Tex's funeral was to be held later that day.

With only a gut-string guitar, the group at the time – Rich Garratt, Brent Burkett, Gary Buck and me – proceeded to learn the melody and lyrics. Later, as we circled the casket and sang, it was all we could do to get through it. By no means was it one of our best performances before that jam-packed congregation, but it was certainly one of our proudest moments. We all loved Tex Ritter, both as a performer and as a person. He helped me and our group in so many ways. Yes, in every sense of the word, we were *FANS*. We were also fans (and friends) of numerous other Country Music Legends who have since passed on to Tex's Hillbilly Heaven. The late Sarah Ophelia Cannon (Minnie Pearl) was first a friend and mentor as we shared cast membership on The Grand Ole Opry. She later became my Aunt by marriage. Again, I was deeply saddened by her death, yet honored to have been a pallbearer at her funeral. Others who have had a major influence in my professional and personal life include: Roy Acuff, Marty Robbins, Faron Young, Ferlin Huskey, George Morgan, Bob Luman, Ernest Tubb, and the great steel guitar player, Pete Drake. Jimmy Dean's influence has already been noted.

You see, when I got into Country Music, it was dominated by older acts. I was but a young *Four Guy* entering a mature entertainment world. In those days, an act's career would go on until the act himself/herself decided the time had come to quit. Sadly I have watched those wonderful Country Music Personalities slowly fade away, but I remain extremely proud to have known and worked with each of them and countless others.

Meantime, back to *YOUR* career. When you find that you do, in fact, have talent and are able to sing and entertain, you will suddenly find that you are building a loyal following. This following can be of special assistance to you and your "Show-Biz" aspirations if both you and they keep things in perspective. At this point, they become fans; people who admire you and your work; people who can help support you in the good times yet can be of even greater importance in helping you through the hungry years.

Sometime in the near future, at least one person will evolve from your new loyal following and for whatever secret motivation will really want to help you succeed. He/she (more often than not *SHE*) will ask to start and run a Fan Club for you. You'll be extremely flattered and will probably grant permission to do so. It's O.K. – no problem yet. Most Fan Clubs and their members are perfectly harmless and can, if guided properly, be of some help while your career is being launched. In fairness, they can also become a gigantic pain in the butt and cause more problems than they help solve.

One way fan club members can hurt an up and coming artist is to persistently call radio stations and their top D.J.'s requesting their favorite artist's latest disc. Stations encourage listener feedback, but remember the earlier words of Big Jack Barlow and/or Joe E. Lewis, "SOMETIMES A FRIEND IN NEED IS A PEST." Personally, I think a fan club's greatest function is keeping your ego fed (morale boosted, if you will) during times when your career is either stalled or is going backwards. During those times, an encouraging word can be a mighty welcomed sound. Also, a club can turn out its' membership in support of a local gig you're about to play and make you a hero with the venue operator. It's especially good fun to mix and mingle with your Fan Club Members during the Super Bowl of Fandom – FAN FAIR.

Now called THE CMA MUSIC FESTIVAL (it will always be Fan Fair to me), this annual assembling of Country Music Fans in Nashville, Tennessee, is a celebration where fans gather, enjoy concerts and festivities for nearly an entire week. The event will without fail attract more than twenty-five thousand official registrants (fans) to Music City. Loudilla, Loretta and Kay Johnson, known to Country Music fans and followers as The Johnson Sisters, started Fan Fair in the early '70's in support of their megastar, Loretta Lynn. In fact, from their home in Wild Horse, Colorado, they created an entire international fan club organization aptly called IFCO. At last count, IFCO had a worldwide membership base exceeding five-hundred fan clubs. Check out their web site at: www.ifco.org. These gals should be considered the perfect models for creating and operating a fan club. They also have proven how very powerful and helpful a club can be while supporting its' star with consideration and class. WSM Radio (home to The Grand Ole Opry) became a co-sponsor of Fan Fair along with The Johnsons. Later, The Country Music Association (CMA) became involved, and for reasons unknown to me and others the girls were pushed aside. The next time the Country Music Hall of Fame committee gets together to consider future nominees, it's my feeling (and I know, HOSS, who cares about my feeling?). The Johnson Sisters should be considered. Over the years, they have contributed a "Hall of Fame Effort" in promoting Country Music around the world.

To answer this chapter's title question Who Needs a Fan Club? I think every artist serious about their career should have one, provided they are willing to participate in the club and offer proper guidance to the members. Incidentally, there are two other rules by which an artist should live when dealing with fan club presidents and members: Rule number one: NEVER, EVER GET ROMANTICALLY INVOLVED. Rule number two: NEVER FORGET RULE NUMBER ONE!

CHAPTER TWELVE
FAMILY LIFE and THE PATH
TO STARDOM

Like drinking and driving, family life and the path to stardom simply don't mix. They don't mix while driving a motor vehicle and more often than not, they don't mix in show business no matter how hard we all try (and yes, I'm including myself in this group of well meaning people). Show folks are very much like spoiled children. We find out early that we have a special talent and begin receiving special treatment by those around us. So it's no surprise when most entertainment aspirants begin to feel like we can handle any set of difficult circumstances we may encounter...because after all, WE'RE SPECIAL!

Balancing a hard driving career and a happy home life (sounds like a contradiction in terms to me) has got to be the ultimate task that an entertainer has to face. First of all, the upwardly mobile career, if being handled properly, will take an artist in the exact opposite direction of a happy home environment, namely THE ROAD! Any veteran entertainer/musician can tell you the pit-falls resulting from lengthy periods of time on the road away from home, but most won't. A majority of "road stories" are X-Rated. If I'm going to be really truthful, I have to admit that most are *Triple* X.

When I first moved to Nashville, I began hearing tales of the road from traveling musicians and roadies. I thought it was just a bunch of bragging "pickers" and their hangers-on trying to impress those of us who had never experienced life as a *ROAD SCHOLAR* with colorful and outlandish stories.

My first serious year of traveling our nation's highways saw our group performing in 240-different cities and towns as an opening act for Hank Williams, Jr. Those were 240-performing nights and did not include the travel days necessary to get to each engagement. Sometimes our Booking Agents would schedule short hops (from one engagement to another). Oftentimes they were not so short. One of our bus drivers (who liked to boast that he invented The Road) joked that we soon would have more miles under our butts than *Mariner 3* which was exploring outer space at the time. He further joked that we would know when we had been gone from home too long when our kids began calling us "Uncle Daddy" and when friends and relatives began wearing silver I.D. bracelets with our names on them (a fad at the time calling attention to those Viet Nam Vets Missing In Action).

Along with the many emotions experienced during extensive roadwork, such as: fatigue, boredom, claustrophobia (sleeping in small bus bunks and living in a cramped vehicle with ten to fifteen people), there is a dangerous emotion called *loneliness*. This feeling can make the best Father or even "Husband of the Year" susceptible to the countless temptations of the road. Celebrities at any level – from Lounge Bands to Super Stars – can and do fall victim to the temptations of adoring fans in the front row or backstage groupies (that's right, Sam…let's not take responsibility for our own short comings…let's say we're all victims and blame the fans and groupies). You know, HOSS, sometimes I like writing with you and sometimes I don't! I think you know which time this is.

At any rate, it takes a very special marriage to survive the hazards of roadwork and travel. A marriage counselor I'm not, but I've learned through personal experience and through the experience of others that one of the keys to not letting a relationship deteriorate is to stay in touch with the home front. Cell phones can certainly be credited with helping marriages of entertainers survive longer. Before they existed, it was much more difficult to maintain a happy home while touring the country.

I should be candid and say that many Road Scholars thoroughly enjoy the night after night excitement of visiting city after city in a "love 'em and leave 'em" style. It's a young, single person's dream come true; like the kid in a candy store syndrome.

Looking back on my own experiences, my advice to an up and comer would be as follows: enjoy your music; enjoy your performances and stage work, including the wonderful camaraderie with your stage mates on and off the planks (a theatre term for stage); enjoy all the good food you'll discover at the many regional restaurants to which you'll be exposed; enjoy the tremendous attention and special favors you'll receive; but always remember to STAY FOCUSED on your career and on your home life (if married or otherwise committed). If you're not married or committed, ENJOY YOUR TIME IN THE CANDY STORE!

In fairness here, it's important to tell you that all problems with "crash and burn" relationships do not involve The Road. Your mate must learn quickly that managing an active career is a full-time job and requires much of your time whether you're working the road or back at home base in Music City, USA. They must understand that you will be invited to - and must often attend – every industry-related function available to you; from "NUMBER ONE SONG PARTIES" to ribbon-cutting ceremonies for a new building on Music Row. You must be visible whenever and wherever there is an event covered by the press, music-related and otherwise.

Your personal partner must further understand that you must mix and mingle with all the beautiful people in the entertainment world without any display of jealousy. The key is to school your companion properly and put forth the necessary effort to help your relationship grow and mature in spite of your place in the entertainment business.

Who knows, maybe you'll be among the lucky few who *ARE* able to balance a career with a home life and achieve the best of both. Latest statistics say that only one in three marriages survive in the normal world. The odds for "Show-Biz" marriages have got to be much greater against marital bliss.Understandably, it's difficult to find a potential partner who is willing to surrender their own identity to become MR. or MRS. COUNTRY MUSIC STAR...even though it pays well.

CHAPTER THIRTEEN
RULES OF ENGAGEMENT

No, this is not a chapter based on a segment of the Uniform Code of Military Justice. But rather, it could be more accurately titled BASIC RULES TO AID IN GETTING TO THE ENGAGEMENT, also known as "the gig." You see, the more you begin to find success (to whatever degree) the more time you'll find yourself riding in cars and vans pulling trailers; riding in motor homes pulling trailers; riding in old buses (with under-carriages usually large enough so that you need not pull a trailer unless you are responsible for lights and sound).

When you are the front man of your own group and begin spending lots of time traveling our nation's interstate system with band members, drivers and roadies, you'll one day find that you are devoting more time to regulating your group member's habits and oversights than you are too working on and perfecting your music. If you're fortunate enough to hire a veteran traveling musician in the beginning, many of your personnel problems will never develop. Most "pickers" and others involved with a road show are generally willing to do your bidding if you (as leader) spell out the rules for them up front...and then enforce them without fail or exception.

The following rules are the results of more than thirty-years of fronting and managing entertainers and other associates in order to develop a well-oiled traveling music machine. I'll begin with the basic rules that each band or group member was given, by me, before becoming an employee. Each was then asked to review the rules on the spot and discuss any item with which he or she was not comfortable. I/we (The Four Guys) were always willing to discuss and explain our rules and regulations but never willing to negotiate or compromise them. I'm sure you'll be adding your own rules as your career progresses but meanwhile, maybe you'll want to consider some of mine/ours to get you started:

1. Absolutely NO illegal drugs or excessive use of alcohol permitted.
2. There is a 30-minute call required for every performance, including rehearsals. Respect and value everyone's time. Don't be late!
3. No Drinking (water O.K.) or smoking on stage at any time.
4. Cleanliness and neat appearance expected for all performances.
5. Do nothing on stage to sacrifice the sound of the vocals or upstage the overall performance, such as exaggerated physical movements or chatter during or between songs. No vulgarity or off-color material is ever to be used on stage.
6. Any and all hotel/motel room charges, including phone charges, are to be settled with the front desk first thing of the morning prior to check-out. NO LONG DISTANCE phone calls are to be billed to your room (phone cards/cell phones have eliminated much of this problem).
7. Save complaints or suggestions for improvement for rehearsals and group meetings.
8. EVERYONE must attend weekly group meeting scheduled to keep lines of communication open with fellow band-mates. All ideas for change or improvement should be presented at that time and should always be presented in the form of suggestions.
9. Play it the same every time (within reason)! When material is learned and all parts – musical and vocal – are locked in, the unit needs to hear it the same way every time (boring yes, but necessary).
10. There are no paid rehearsals.
11. All rehearsals are closed (no wives, girlfriends, kids, etc.).
12. Try to leave any and all personal problems at home.

13. Try to smile and support the unit on stage – learn the ways of the group and adapt (you're among friends).
14. There can be absolutely no outside interests that conflict with personal appearances or scheduled rehearsals (when exceptions are made for one, all are entitled).
15 Transportation and rooms are always provided. Food and beverage discounts are obtained when possible.
16. When in doubt about anything, please ask.

Assuming your career reaches the point where you're able to afford and operate a customized bus, you will soon find the need for additional rules and regulations to cover this part of your life on the road. The following top ten hit parade of rules worked well for our organization:

1. No females on the bus at anytime (exceptions for family and for female band members and their female friends). This is your home away from home – treat it as such.
2. All clothes and luggage is to be stowed away and out of sight at all times. All bags and suitcases too large to fit under or in bunks are to be stored in under-carriage of bus.
3. Help keep the bus clean by emptying your share of ashtrays (in hiring practice preference is always given non-smokers) and placing newspapers, soft drink cans and fast food containers in trash bins.
4. Shut your bunk curtains when not in bunk so that aisle-ways look orderly.
5. Clean your bunk at the conclusion of each engagement.
6. Keep traffic in sleeping areas to a minimum and socializing/partying to times when others are not trying to sleep.
7. Participate in night rotation schedule so that there is a "shotgun" rider with driver at all times. If you feel the driver is speeding, getting drowsy or acting in some other unusual manner that could create a safety hazard, alert the other group members immediately.
8. Fuel and rest stops are to be kept to approximately 30 minutes.
9. Keep each other informed of whereabouts at all stops so that no one is left at a stop. It's a good idea to call the roll before leaving a rest/fuel stop.

Before we were able to employ a Bus Driver, we all shared driving chores in four hour or 200 mile legs.

Originally, we each drove 200 miles. That was amended to four hours or 200 miles, WHICHEVER comes first. You see, I got stuck on a 200 mile leg from the Pacific Ocean to Redding, California. All well and good except that I hadn't realized the entire trip was through the mountains and took the better part of seven-hours to make. By a vote of One To Nothing (the other guys were sleeping so I didn't ask them to vote), I amended the driving rule to include four hours OR 200 miles whichever came first.

When the time comes that you can afford a professional driver, the following guidelines for that position might prove helpful:

1. Vehicle to be cleaned, fueled, washed and serviced prior to all road trips (assuming it's YOUR bus and not one provided by a leasing company). Specifically, head(s) are to be cleaned and emptied. Water tank should be emptied and filled with fresh water just prior to the next trip. Towel and toilet tissue racks should be re-stocked.

2. Interior head(s), trash cans and aisle-way to be cleaned upon arrival at engagement site or prior to leaving for next date or return trip.

3. Driver to remain with vehicle during all pit stops until servicing is completed.

4. Oil, tires and batteries to be checked at all pit stops.

5. Driver to see that all passengers are aboard before leaving fuel/rest stops.

6. Never let a diesel engine run low or out of fuel. Never let a diesel engine lug or idle. Diesels are meant to run, not putt.

7. When not driving, driver is to be sleeping or otherwise getting rest.

8. There are absolutely NO ILLEGAL DRUGS in this organization (worth repeating).

9. The Driver should map out the entire trip in advance and keep an accurate log.

10. DRIVER PAYS FOR ALL TRAFFIC TICKETS (this solves any potential speeding problems).

CHAPTER FOURTEEN
YOUR CAREER –
YOUR CELEBRITY
(respect them both)

No matter what we do in life, we all want a little respect. Whether we're Sanitary Engineers (trash collectors), world renowned Surgeons or Rodney Dangerfield, we want and need a small "pat on the back" every now and then. It's my belief that all God's children have at least some small traits for which they would like to be recognized. Those perfections – large or small – and the accolades they bring are clearly two separate areas with which a person must deal and control. Any appreciation and recognition for the bright side of a particular personality should be regarded as friendly in nature and handled with a tremendous amount of care and affection.

As a young professional entertainer, your entire focus will surely be geared toward developing your career. As that development occurs, a certain degree of celebrity will begin to evolve. You will most likely embrace that celebrity as your "pat on the back" and enjoy all the good things it brings your way. Being recognized as you walk down the street and approached for autographs is certainly a wonderful feeling in the beginning. It's important to remember those early feelings of acceptance and special treatment as your career progresses and you find yourself living in a very public arena. Should your career really take off and you become the subject of everybody's conversation, you will need all the tolerance you can muster to deal with the public's attention. Suddenly you're famous. Just as suddenly, your career and your celebrity become separate entities, yet they are bound together by the music you make and the persona you project.

At this point, your career should be guided and advanced with the help of those in your organization who are schooled in strategic planning. These people will decide what public events you should attend; what TV show invitations you should accept; what press and magazine interviews should be scheduled; and all the other ways and means with which to enhance your public image. Along with providing your input in all these areas, you will need to concentrate heavily on helping your record producer choose just the right material for your next recording sessions.

How do you deal with your growing celebrity while taking part in all those other career areas just mentioned? So long as you keep things in perspective, managing your celebrity is the easiest part of your "Show-Biz" life. In fact, if handled properly, your fame can provide you and yours a great living long after your days of recording hit records have passed.

That said; analyze the Country Music careers of George Jones, Dolly Parton, Johnny Cash, Charley Pride, Hank Williams, Jr., Loretta Lynn, Emmy Lou Harris, Eddy Arnold, Marty Robbins, Mel Tillis, Reba McIntyre, and The Oak Ridge Boys.

Then look at the Contemporary Music and the Hollywood careers of Elvis Presley, Bob Hope, Elizabeth Taylor, Frank Sinatra, Dean Martin, Barbara Streisand, Wayne Newton, Sammy Davis Jr., Paul Anka, George Burns, Jack Benny, John Wayne, and Katharine Hepburn.

In nearly every career just mentioned, the hit records and movies have long since passed. In fact, many of these famous people are deceased, yet their celebrity continues to grow. Why? Because in life, most of them embraced their fame and learned to create images for themselves which are interesting, provocative, controversial and oftentimes outlandish. They didn't hide from the paparazzi − they subtly sought them out and were never intimidated by a flash bulb or a camera.

In the beginning, it's CAREER and CELEBRITY — equal parts rolled into one gratifying experience. A little later, it's CAREER and CELEBRITY separating, forming distinctly different identities; each one requiring special attention to work in concert with the other. Still later (if you make it this far), CELEBRITY takes over and becomes the ENTIRE CAREER.

I think this school of thought can best be explained by simply suggesting that you try to be as excited about signing an autograph after a string of hits as you were when you began your career. Remember when you were first recognized walking down the street in your hometown? Treat that experience as though it happened last week and don't ever forget the recipe for HUMBLE PIE.

CHAPTER FIFTEEN
WHO AM I?

As you begin to develop your music and stage act, you'll find your personality also begins to change. Knowing you have to become Mr. Nice Guy/Gal to win more and more adoring fans, you'll suddenly find (if you're in touch with your true feelings) that you are rapidly becoming a somewhat different person. You're no longer allowed to have bad days. Everyone will always expect you to be up, happy, positive and accommodating. Remember? It's "Show-Biz." Phony as a three-dollar bill, but that's just the way it is, and the sooner you buy into it the better off you'll become. Grumpy old entertainers simply do not attract the masses the way beaming personalities do.

Problems start to arise when your new business personality comes in conflict with your true self and you begin to flounder in a clouded world of confusion. The key is to find a spot that doesn't take you too far from the real you and allows you to walk freely in both show business and the real world. Where is that spot? Only you can begin to seek it out and develop it. I'm merely making you aware of the probable scenarios that are sure to occur so that you can prepare yourself and adapt.

Some entertainers I know have gotten so phony so fast that they lose track of who they are and actually become a whole new person; oftentimes, it is not a very good person. A small amount of success has been known to cause serious damage to both personal and peer relationships. There's an old saying in this business which proposes that we should be nice to those we meet on the way up because we're likely to see them again on the way down.

In the late '60's, when I was a struggling group singer, I began to chum around with a young struggling songwriter who was one of the nicest guys I'd met in Nashville. We would joke together; rabbit hunt together and drink beer together at Tootsie's Orchid Lounge (which was really our favorite hobby). So tremendous was his writing ability that he quickly became noticed by the Music Community. Consequently HIS struggle didn't last very long. He rapidly joined the ranks of Country Music's top songwriters. In addition, he became a major recording artist, turning out many big, big hits of his own music.

Due to conflicting schedules, our paths didn't cross again for about a year. Then one night backstage at a package show (a show featuring multiple acts) we were both working, we passed each other. Happy for his huge success, I excitedly yelled out his name and asked him how he was doing. Without stopping, he looked at me like he wasn't sure who I was and then said, "EVERYTHING'S FINE MAN" and kept on walking the other direction. This was my first exposure to just how serious success can change people. It was my first exposure but certainly not the last and my own personality grew for the better as a result. These learning experiences taught me exactly how NOT to become when and if success ever came my way. I can't emphasize enough the need to keep your feet on the ground and your head out of the clouds if your career begins to grow and by all means, don't EVER take yourself so seriously that you start to believe your inflated biography and glowing press clippings.

A genuine sense of humor goes a long way toward maintaining sanity while helping you sustain your real personality. Remember I said earlier that I thought songwriters were some of the best people to hang out with in the Music Business? That is because most writers have great senses of humor and are fun to be around.

I ran into a writer buddy of mine awhile back and asked him if he'd written any good material lately. He said yes – he'd just written a monster hit called, *"I GOT YOU OUT OF MY MIND, NOW IF I CAN JUST GET YOU OUT OF MY CONDO."* He added that he had recently written two more songs entitled "*I'VE GOT TO GET*

BETTER TO DIE" AND*"I'M SO FAR DOWN I'VE GOT TO LOOK UP TO SEE THE GROUND."*

Like I said previously, songwriters see things differently from us so-called "normal" folk." I have learned so much from writers about life – good and bad – in the Music Business. They are truly the life-blood of the industry and deserve far more credit than they ever receive. That doesn't seem to be a problem for any of the writers I have ever known; at least not with regard to the type of credit we are speaking of here. Most writers are not really interested in the things the rest of us set out to accomplish, such as fame and fortune. Sure, they want and hope to get "THEIR DUE" in time, but they seem to be more interested in assembling the greatest set of lyrics ever written to couple with the most original melody ever heard. Result? The SONG of the CENTURY. They are far more interested in receiving an award from their peers in publishing, licensing and their own Songwriter's Association than they are in receiving an accolade from a fan, artist or record company.

I would have to say that songwriters can answer the question, *WHO AM I* better than anyone else in the business. Most writers that I have met are real people who know exactly who they are and what they are attempting to achieve.

While you are deciding how to adjust your new show business personality so that you are able to retain much of your true self, it would be wise to study the ways of writers and try to capture their ability to make their way around Music Row while retaining their TRUE identity.

When all is said and done, you will most certainly want to end up telling your grandchildren who you are and who you were. You will have had great success if both are one and the same!

CHAPTER SIXTEEN
MUSIC IMMORTALITY

If a long-lasting career is not enough for you and you are eager to create a legacy of immortality (what an ego), you should begin immediately to hone your songwriting skills. Writing hit songs is as close as you'll ever get to winning the respect of future music generations. No matter how much talent we have as singers, performers and musicians, we'll only be as big as our last hit recording or our most recent national or international achievement (such as performing the National Anthem at a Super Bowl). In Nashville, the saying goes "IT ALL BEGINS WITH A SONG." We should amend that to say, "IT ENDS THERE AS WELL." Songwriters (as I've already noted) make up the most unusual and complex segment of our music community. That's being as kind as I can be to a group of folks who think and say things much differently from the majority. I once heard that the difference between a COMIC and a COMEDIAN is that a COMIC says funny things – a COMEDIAN says things funny. The difference between "GOOD" and "GREAT" songwriters is that "GOOD" songwriters have a normal vision of life around them while "GREAT" tunesmiths see and say things in the abstract or in a most unusual fashion.

Personally, I would consider myself to be an average songwriter. I have written many songs over the years and have even had a few recorded. But without fail, whenever I'm in the presence of a true songwriter (and you learn to spot them in a crowd), I realize I can never play in their league. I'm a "Double A" player at best. Most of these guys and gals are "Major League" all the way.

Along with being tremendously rewarding, songwriting is probably the most frustrating existence in the music industry. It seems everybody is a songwriter in Nashville (or at least aspires to be). Those who have made it (i.e. those who have written songs which have become hits) say it's an effort you must work at every day in order to even have a chance at success. One veteran artist who hit a homerun by becoming successful as both a performer and a songwriter is Tom T. Hall. He is reported to have once said that you've got to write a hundred bad songs before you write a good one. In other words, if you hope to succeed, you better get started and get that first hundred out of the way.

Country Music Legend Tex Ritter (mentioned earlier) was co-hosting The Ralph Emery All-Night Radio Show on WSM in 1967 when I first met him. Our group had dropped in on Ralph (customary in those days) to plug our very first record – SHENANDOAH. It was a pleasant surprise to meet and talk to Tex (or Mr. Ritter, as we rightfully called him that night). We had just arrived in Nashville from the Wheeling, West Virginia Jamboree (an Opry type show broadcast on WWVA Radio – a 50-thousand watt powerhouse station that covers most of the northeastern part of the United States and much of Canada). It seems Tex had performed on the Jamboree many times over the years and immediately began a conversation with us about several of the show's regulars. Instantaneously, there was an immediate attraction to and an admiration for this wonderful man. I remember him saying at one point, "you boys are new in the business; learn to write songs. They'll be around long after you're gone. A lifetime of checks coming in for you and your family is not hard to take either." It was good advice that didn't really work out for any of *us,* but advice that can, will and has for countless others.

Let me relate a couple of isolated instances where songwriting has really paid off. The songwriting team of Helen Darling and Billy Montana has written hundreds of songs and has gotten many of those songs (thru their publisher) placed with major and not so major artists. Reportedly, they were squeezing out a living practicing their craft when they finally got a song placed on Jo Dee Messina's third career album called *BURN*. The song was called *BRING ON THE RAIN* and almost never got released as a single. Finally, as the fourth SINGLE release from the album, it was "*RAIN'S*" turn. Three years after Darling and Montana wrote it, *BRING ON THE RAIN* hit NUMBER ONE on Billboard Magazine and Radio and Records charts. To reach Number One status, a record needs to get to the top of either − but preferably both − charts.

With more than 2,000 Country Radio Stations playing the song, an initial payday was reported of $1,000,000 in Broadcast Royalties alone. This did not include foreign royalties nor anything from the sale of the single or the album. Sales from albums are tallied separately. Getting one song on an album selling 1.2 million copies (which *BURN did* at the time of this reporting) would net eight cents per song, per record sold. This amount would then be split between the publishers and the writers.

In the case of *BRING ON THE RAIN*, all those with ownership and publishing rights would split about $95,000. And this was only the beginning. Before it had a complete run (and there's really no such thing as a complete run, to be explained later), BURN and BRING ON THE RAIN will have brought many large paydays to the writers and publisher(s). Publishers, like Talent Agencies, oftentimes cut deals whereby publishing rights are split with other companies in order to get a song recorded by a major artist. A close personal friend and publisher was a part of just such a deal, where there were four companies involved in the publishing of a Conway Twitty hit and the title song of a subsequent album (record labels used to get a hit single first, then record an album with the single's title).

My friend and his one-quarter publishing rights have received and continue to receive substantial royalty payments from the sale and airing of that one hit song by Conway Twitty − This after more than 25 years from the date of its' original release. MUSIC IMMORTALITY? Not yet, but getting closer.

One final word about songwriters; along with having a magic way with words and music, most (as I've said) have a tremendous sense of humor. One of Music Row's finest once asked me if I knew how to get a Songwriter off your front porch? I said I didn't know.

He replied, "PAY HIM/HER FOR THE PIZZA!" Of course, this was recalling the hungry years that most experience!

*** The Tennessean Newspaper – Nashville's only major daily publication – is the source used for the aforementioned recording and publishing information***

Welcome To Nashville – Home of the Grand Ole Opry

(Photo by Eddie Malone)

RYMAN AUDITORIUM: This historic building located in downtown Nashville served as the home of the Grand Ole Opry from 1943-1974.

GRAND OLE OPRY HOUSE: Located at Opryland USA, this ultra-modern show facility seats approximately 4,400 and spotlights Opry performances on Friday and Saturday nights. (Photos by Eddie Malone and used by permission of Gaylord Entertainment Company)

COUNTRY MUSIC HALL OF FAME: The all new and greatly enlarged building welcomes tourists and historians to downtown Nashville throughout the year. (Photo by Eddie Malone)

BROADCAST MUSIC, INC. (BMI) and the AMERICAN SOCIETY
OF COMPOSERS, AUTHORS and PUBLISHERS (ASCAP) are two
of the music industry's largest licensing entities. Nashville offices
are located in the Music Row area. (Photos by Eddie Malone)

NASHVILLE ASSOCIATION OF MUSICIANS: Local #257 boasts a membership of approximately three-thousand (3000).

AMERICAN FEDERATION OF TELEVISION and RADIO ARTISTS (AFTRA) has merged with the SCREEN ACTORS GUILD (SAG) and the combined Unions continue to grow as they serve the entertainment community's singers, broadcasters and actors. (Photos by Eddie Malone)

BUDDY LEE ATTRACTIONS, founded in the late '60's by its' namesake, former wrestler Buddy Lee, was established primarily to handle the career of Hank Williams, Jr. It has since grown into one of Nashville's largest talent agencies. (Photo by Eddie Malone)

STUDIO "A": During the '50's and '60's, Studio A was one of Nashville's premier recording studios, while hosting countless record sessions by the city's music elite, most notably ELVIS PRESLEY. (Photo by Eddie Malone)

SONY RECORDS and MUSIC PUBLISHING: One of several music conglomerates now operating on or near the Music Row area.

TYPICAL MUSIC ROW PUBLISHING HOUSE: Like most, this one boasting banners of recent hit songs. (Photos by Eddie Malone)

SAMPLING OF MUSIC ROW AREA HOUSING: A typical example of facilities available for lease or rent. Rental costs are relatively inexpensive. (Photo by Eddie Malone)

SHOWCASE CLUBS: frequented by Nashville music newcomers, showcase clubs such as Tootsie's Orchid Lounge has served as both local hangouts and launching pads for major Country Music Stars through the years, including headliner Terri Clark, who is said to have performed regularly for tips.

ROBERT'S WESTERN WORLD: down the street from Tootsie's, Robert's is another popular hangout. Robert's advertises itself as the home of BR549, a talented group of musicians and singers who scored several hit albums in the late '90's. (Photos by Eddie Malone)

THE NASHVILLE PALACE is located across from The Opryland Hotel at Opryland, and has been a popular Nashville night spot for more than 20 years. Randy Travis once worked as a dishwasher here and did guest spots on stage during his evening breaks. (Photo by Eddie Malone)

ORIGINAL ERNEST TUBB RECORD SHOP: Located on Broadway in downtown Nashville, the shop once hosted the famed MIDNIGHT JAMBOREE, a free show aired immediately after the Grand Old Opry broadcast on WSM Radio. (Photo by Eddie Malone)

Shows are now aired at the new Ernest Tubb Record Shop and Theatre on Music Valley Drive in the Opryland Hotel area. (Photo by Eddie Malone)

Grand Ole Opry

THE FOUR GUYS

BUDDY LEE

Exclusive Management
BUDDY LEE ATTRACTIONS, Inc.
806 16th Avenue, South
Nashville, Tenn. 37203
A/C 615   244-4336

ORIGINAL FOUR GUY'S PROMOTIONAL PHOTO:
taken for the group's first appearance in the official Grand
Ole Opry Picture History Book, marketed internationally
and at each Opry performance. (Photo by Les Leverett)

FINAL PROMOTIONAL PHOTO of THE FOUR GUYS: used until the group's original members, Sam Wellington and Brent Burkett (first and third from left, respectively) retired in 1999. (Photo by Eddie Malone)

HOSS NOBODY: alter ego and writing companion of
author Sam Wellington. (Photo by Eddie Malone)

CHAPTER SEVENTEEN
IS THE PIE BIG ENOUGH?

The more successful you become, the bigger your organization will grow. As you begin to calculate your ongoing obligations, you might start to wonder "will there be anything left for me?" The mere hint of success will draw hangers-on like a moth to a flame (isn't that a line from a Jim Reeves hit?). Thank you HOSS for pointing out my lack of creativity. By the way "smart butt," what was that hit?

Let's have some fun and dream positively for a while. Let's assume you have made your move to Nashville, gotten a job, started displaying your singing, writing and performing wares all over town and in a relatively short period of time landed a major record deal. Right out of the chute, you score three top ten hits in a row. Your fourth record achieves NUMBER ONE status. Suddenly, you're in the BIG MONEY (how do you like this dream so far?). Just as suddenly, you'll find yourself surrounded by a Personal Manager, a Talent Agent, a Business Manager, a Public Relations Representative, a Road Manager, a Hair/Makeup person, a five or six-piece Backup Band, Sound and Lights People, a Bus Driver(s), not one but two customized buses and a couple of "Roadies/Gofers" (it's still a little soon for your own airplane). So far, I haven't mentioned record company promotion people and publishing reps; though not directly related to your immediate payroll, they are still in your camp earning big dollars from your recording efforts.

Unless you're able to keep a close eye on things, it will very quickly seem like every one but YOU is getting a piece of YOUR pie. That was the feeling we got at the peak of our career, even without big hit records. As an example of what can happen with a career built solely on stage performance, I/we had a payroll of fifty-one people (including those employed at our Four Guy's Harmony House Theatre-Restaurant in Nashville during the years 1975-85), along with a five-piece band, two buses, a van, drivers, a sound/lights crew and roadies. Amidst all this were the usual Personal Manager, Booking Agent, CPA, and two Bookkeepers. We had lots of problems in those last two areas over the years.

At this point, a quote from a friend and former Landlord Jack Greer might be in order. Jack owned and operated Greer's Cafeteria at 407 Murfreesboro Road in Nashville for more than 20 years. After having his fill of the restaurant business, he decided to close and lease the building and property, both of which he owned outright. On July 18th, 1975, The Four Guys signed a ten-year lease/purchase agreement for the property and launched *The Harmony House Theatre-Restaurant* a month later. How do I remember that date so well? Our Tenor Singer at the time, Gary Buck, married Louise Mandrell of The Mandrell Sisters (name-dropping again?) the same day and had to rush his wedding in order to get to our attorney's office in time for the lease signing.

Meanwhile, back to the Jack Greer quote. He once said, "lock the back door. Employees will carry it out the back faster than you can bring it in the front." He added, "employees should be considered GUILTY until proven INNOCENT." Jack became a little cynical in his later years (to say the least) and his philosophy was directed towards restaurant/club people. Nevertheless, his words could easily be applied to other areas, including the entertainment field. For instance, "LOCK THE BACK DOOR" could very well apply to keeping your eye on the books and those in charge of YOUR MONEY. The good news is there are ways and means of dealing with problems which arise at YOUR BACK DOOR.

The best method I've found is to build your organization with special care and attention given to quality and establish a system with plenty of checks and balances independent of TRUST. If your system works properly, you won't have to worry quite as much about trusting those who are running it. Keep your eye on the ball at all times. Regular meetings with regular accounting practices will insure you that there WILL be a piece of the pie left for you after everyone else is paid. To emphasize further, remember to always keep your thumb IN the pie and not merely on it. My Dear Ole Daddy used to say, "take care of your business and your business will take care of you (come on, Wellington…are you sure you want to use the DEAR OLE DADDY line here?)." HOSS, I'm not only gonna use that line (which is true) but I'm gonna use a line yelled out to me from an audience member one night during a stage show. I made a huge mistake by asking if anyone in the audience had any requests. A guy yelled out, "YEAH, TAKE A BREAK." So HOSS, isn't it about time for YOU to go to lunch?

We began this chapter with a little positive dreaming. It is my sincere hope that the hit record portion of the dream comes true for you and that the other portions (business-related) do not turn into a NIGHTMARE.

CHAPTER EIGHTEEN
FOR THE RECORD

No matter what level of success you achieve in the music field, you will always need to keep accurate records. Sure, the more successful you become, the more help you will have available to you. Nevertheless, it's up to you in the beginning to put the pieces of the puzzle together in order to eventually create the smoothly running entertainment machine that I talked about earlier.

The following forms you will need outline four of the areas on which you should concentrate: (1) ROAD CHECKLIST (2) PERFORMANCE GUIDE (3) STAGE PLOT/SETUP and (4) TOUR(S) ITINERARY. #1. A "Road Checklist" should be prepared well in advance of an impending tour or single night engagement and distributed to all members of your organization. Here's a sample of what I used for many years:

Sam Wellington

ENGAGEMENT: _____

DATE(S): _____   SHOW SITE: _____

SHOWTIME(S): _____   LENGTH OF SHOW(S) _____

REPORT: _____   SET-UP TIME: _____

SOUND CHECK: _____   REHEARSAL: _____

TRANSPORTATION: BUS _____ AIR _____   OTHER _____

DRIVER: _____   CONTACTED BY: _____

AIRLINE RESERVATIONS MADE BY: _____   DATE: _____

RENTAL CAR(S) RESERVED BY: _____   DATE: _____

OTHER TRAVEL DETAILS: _____

HOTEL RESERVATIONS MADE BY: _____   DATE: _____

HOTEL LOCATION: _____

HOTEL CONTACT: _____

PHONE NUMBER: _____

NUMBER OF ROOMS: _____   DATES BOOKED: _____

ROOM ASSIGNMENTS: _____

OVERNIGHT: _____   CLEAN UP: _____   IN WHOSE NAME: _____

OTHER PERTINENT DETAILS: _____

SOUND and LIGHTING REQUIREMENTS: _____

IF WE PROVIDE, DO WE HAVE: Board _____   Speakers _____

Monitors _____   Amps _____   Mics/Stands _____   Cords and Connectors _____

CD Player/Cassette Deck _____   Recorded Show Material _____

(Tracks, misc.) _____   Show Props _____

RECORDED PROMOTIONAL AND FOR SALE PRODUCT: _____

PHOTOGRAPHS: _____   PRESS KITS: _____

OTHER DETAILS: _____

Form Number #2. I found that having a PERFORMANCE GUIDE detailing everything imaginable about each approaching engagement was very useful and a worthwhile tool for our organization (band, etc…). It is especially helpful for return engagements, when a quick glance at your file will re-familiarize you with any special or unusual quirks about the venue. Here again is a sample of what worked well for me:

SHOW SITE LOCATION AND NAME:

SHOW SITE SPECIFICS: (a) Seating Capacity:

(b) Pertinent Sound Info:

(c) Pertinent Lighting Info:

(d) Show Format   Shows # _____   Dance _____

Other _____

(e) Rooms Provided: _____   How Many _____

(f) Food and Beverage Discounts:

(g) Performance Times:

(h) Buyer/Show Room/Arena Manager's Name _____
Address and Phone Number:

AGENCY COMMISSIONS NOT TO BE WITHHELD BY BUYER:

DISTANCE TO SHOW SITE FROM NASHVILLE:

DISTANCE FROM SHOW SITE TO NEXT SHOW SITE:

BORDER CROSSING ARRANGEMENTS (work permits, passports, etc.)

ABILITY TO SELL CONCESSIONS (CD's, Tapes, T-Shirts, Hats, etc.

(NOTE: All large venues and many smaller ones will charge a commission, sometimes as much as 30 percent, on your product sales. This often is negotiable.)

(Performance Guide continued…)

FOR MULTI-NITE ENGAGEMENTS (sit-down gigs): Showroom must be available to act for use for at least three (3) hours daily for rehearsal and sound checks: _____
METHOD OF PAYMENT: (NOTE: There is usually a 50 percent deposit 30 days prior to date, with the remainder paid upon completion of engagement): _____
COMMISSION PERCENTAGE: _____ Payable to: _____

MEDIA INTERVIEWS SET: (a) Radio _____
                 (b) Radio _____
                 (c) Television _____
                 (d) Newspaper _____
                 (e) Magazine _____

*FOOTNOTE: Always attempt to negotiate gratis (free) rooms along with food and beverage discounts for yourself and your group.

Finally, if you have an adequate lighting system or the venue where you will be performing has one, each song, medley or skit should have its own chart arranged in the order that your stage show is to be presented. The following chart worked well for me through the years and was designed by The Grand Ole Opry's longtime Lighting Director, Suzie Ray:

SONG TITLE: _____
COLOR WASHES:
FRONTLIGHTS: _____
SIDELIGHTS: _____
BACKLIGHTS: _____
DOWNLIGHTS: _____
SPECIALS: _____
FOLLOW SPOTS (bright spotlight(s) placed near rear/sides of venue):
1. _____
2. _____
3. _____

STAGE PLOT/SET-UP

Create a diagram of your specific stage needs, such as the location of the DRUMS, GUITAR(S), KEYBOARDS, FIDDLE(S), EXTRA PERCUSSION INSTRUMENTS, and BACKUP SINGERS. Indicate the stage size required (25 X 25 is usually more than adequate), the Number of Electrical Outlets needed, the Number of Drum Riser(s), and Steps to and from the audience.

ADDITIONAL INFORMATION: _____

Making sure this chart and any other sound requirements you may have gets to the proper channels as soon as possible prior to your scheduled performance will greatly enhance your chances for a successful day/evening on stage. These forms are the necessary tools for your "music machine" to maximize its full potential and bring about positive results. By using them, you can achieve the very best stage show possible and thereby advance your reputation as a professional entertainer.

Following every performance, it's a good idea to make notes on your applicable forms and file them for future use.

Finally, there is a very important fourth form to be considered. The creation of an ITINERARY for every tour or extended engagement is essential. The itinerary should contain departure dates and times, venue location(s), hotel names, locations and phone numbers. Place this in the hands of everyone associated with the tour as far in advance as possible. Copies can be made and left with members on the HOME FRONT (wives, girlfriends, friends and other family members), thereby keeping ALL lines of communication open. A good itinerary will save you lots of time and eliminate the frustration caused from having to answer countless questions your group members will pose prior to and during road trips. Bottom line? GOOD RECORDS are always important, both on the radio *and* in your PERFORMANCE FILE.

CHAPTER NINETEEN
OFF THE RECORD

Long before there was a hit television show called *SURVIVOR*, there were thousands of aspiring actors, actresses, songwriters and musicians trying to survive on the entertainment islands of New York, Nashville and Los Angeles.

Each one has a very unique story to tell, whether or not he or she ever became successful. There is so much to be learned from these gallant pioneers who have already taken their leaps of faith and begun their quests to reach entertainment stardom.

In the following pages, I will briefly discuss some of the necessary ingredients that go into our Pot-O'-Gold Recipe. In addition to providing some helpful hints and shortcuts, I will also touch upon the topics of relationships and politics.

I mentioned earlier the need to get a job, find affordable housing and obtain adequate transportation (paid for) ASAP upon arriving in Nashville. You must also find ways and means to get your talent in front of as many people as possible. Showcase Clubs are a good place to start, but getting in front of the masses is also necessary. This means volunteering for benefits such as telethons and special events covered by the Nashville news media. Showing your face at any positive and noteworthy event can help get your name in the paper and your face and voice on radio and television.

National talent shows have become a way for instant recognition. First, there was *STAR SEARCH* in the '80's and '90's, on which the group SAWYER BROWN was one of the big winners. The network show AMERICAN IDOL has produced several hit acts, including RUBEN STUDDARD, CLAY AIKEN, KELLY CLARKSTON, and a Nashville area singer, KIMBERLY LOCKE. Another show called *NASHVILLE STAR* saw both the singing and writing talents of *BUDDY JEWELL* skyrocket to national stardom. I'm sure Buddy would not agree with the term "skyrocket," after beating around Nashville studios and clubs for more than ten-years prior to his appearance on the show. Nevertheless, he entered the local contest in December of 2002 and went on to win out over eight-thousand contestants from coast to coast by May of 2003. By August of the same year, he and SONY MUSIC had a hit album (produced by Clint Black) containing the hit single, LACI'S SONG, and others. So, are talent shows a vehicle to explore? I would say absolutely. Exposure gained from these shows and others has landed major record deals for many artists, even though they DIDN'T WIN the grand prize.

On that note, some of the best advice I/we ever received was to "LEARN OUR NATIONAL ANTHEM." We did and sang it countless times at local and national sporting events for many years. It gave our group wide exposure that we would have never received. One such special time was the 80th birthday celebration of our friend, mentor and hero, Roy Acuff. The event was held at The Grand Ole Opry House and was attended by several thousand people, including the President of the United States at the time, Ronald Reagan.

We also were called upon numerous times by The Opry and CMA to sing the anthem to open the annual Fan Fair festivities. Twenty-five-thousand-plus Country Music enthusiasts made up the audience. Forty-one-thousand sports fans (many in the music community) cheered us on time and again as we sang the anthem prior to Vanderbilt University football games. An even greater number stood and watched us on national TV as we performed our nation's song prior to a Chicago Cubs game at Wrigley Field in Chicago. Still another national audience saw our performance just prior to THE HALL of FAME BOWL in Birmingham, Alabama.

There are often hazards associated with performing live in major arenas and outdoor stadiums. Because of the enormity of the venues, there are usually two-to- three-second delays from the time your voice enters your microphone to the time the sound comes out of the large, highly elevated speakers. It's very confusing to sing while hearing your voice a couple of seconds later.

Also, you'll be working with stadium sound equipment which has been known to fail now and again. That is exactly what happened to us one night at Greer Stadium in Nashville, just prior to a Nashville Sounds baseball game. We were about to sing when we heard a loud "POP." Not knowing that the system had just imploded, we began with, "OH SAY CAN YOU SEE" and proceeded to sing through the entire anthem a cappella without a sound system. Our Opry Buddy Johnny Russell was in the stands and later told us, IT WAS THE BEST HE "NEVER" HEARD.

I think I've made my point - LEARN OUR NATIONAL ANTHEM - but do a thorough sound check prior to your performance. Learning the anthem is not only a nice patriotic thing to do (especially in these times), but it's one of the greatest promotional tools you'll ever develop. One more thing: When performing the National Anthem, try to be original with your vocal arrangement, yet preserve the original melody to whatever extent you can. I've heard many singers obliterate the melody while trying to display their own unique style. The idea is to sing the fire out of it without having Francis Scott Key (the writer) turn over in his grave.

Remember I said earlier that people in Nashville help their friends? So it's obvious that you need to develop as many relationships as possible. You can't have too many friends in this city. How do you accomplish this? Get out and about on Music Row. Bang on as many doors (in a friendly manner) as you can. Talk to people. Eat at MEAT 'N THREES, such as THE PIE WAGON, ARNOLDS, BROWN'S DINER and others. There's a side benefit to this; the food is good and reasonably priced. Most importantly, don't sit around your lonely apartment waiting for the phone to ring. YOU'VE got to make the phone ring. You'll be amazed at your progress once you start building friendships; that is of course assuming you have the talent and ability with which to progress.

Let me tell you about a very talented bass guitar player who joined our back-up band in the '70's. His name is Buddy Cannon. I met Buddy and his friend Steve Smith (a fellow guitar player) in Las Vegas during an engagement at The Landmark Hotel with –

among others – Grand Ole Opry Star Bob Luman. Buddy and Steve were not only talented musicians but were great guys as well. They worked with Bob Luman through his most successful years until his untimely death in the early '70's. We invited both Buddy and Steve to join our back-up band and both became wonderful assets. Steve later left to join The Gatlin Brothers where he remained for a dozen years or more. Buddy was unhappy working the road and eventually left to pursue a songwriting career. This meant some hungry times while he began plugging songs for the Mel Tillis Publishing Company, SAWGRASS MUSIC, during which time he developed many important relationships with the people on Music Row.

Probably the most important of those was when Buddy met Harold Shedd. Harold, at the time, was one of the most successful Record Producers in Country Music. He was responsible for most of the hits produced on the group Alabama. He also discovered and produced K.T. Oslin and The Kentucky Headhunters (two successful acts of the early '90's) while being instrumental in the achievements of Billy Ray Cyrus and a host of others. Harold is reported to have said that he liked Buddy Cannon immediately and especially admired his honesty. It seems Buddy would oftentimes present Harold with what he thought would be a good song for Alabama, even though he (Buddy) had no ties to the song and stood to gain nothing financially.

It was this relationship that led Buddy to expose his own writing and producing skills leading him to become one of the city's top writer/producers, eventually working with Toby Keith, Sammy Kershaw, George Jones and many others.

Buddy Cannon is a glowing example of the many good things that can happen when friendships are created and nurtured OFF THE RECORD. His talent and determination were also instrumental in his ability to not only *SURVIVE* but *PROSPER* on this entertainment island called MUSIC CITY, USA.

CHAPTER TWENTY
ODDS ARE...

What better segment to discuss the odds of success than CHAPTER THIRTEEN? My original outline called for thirteen chapters, but I decided to add others so as not to end on such an unlucky number and wait until much later (chapter twenty) to discuss the odds of YOUR SUCCESS. I'm usually not very superstitious, but have you ever noticed that most hotels do not have a thirteenth floor? If Conrad Hilton is concerned enough to skip a floor for fear of bad luck, I should at least give all possibilities some consideration. I couldn't tell this story in thirteen chapters anyway (Sammy, do you really think this is THE GREATEST STORY EVER TOLD?). Hello again, HOSS. I see you're back from lunch.

The first thing a person attempting to break into the Music Business should realize is that the odds of success will never be in your favor. Even with the information contained herein coupled with all that you uncover on your own, you'll be fighting the odds at every turn. I don't say this to scare you off or frighten you from taking your shot. However, I cannot emphasize enough the harsh reality of what's facing you and I want you to always be mindful of the battles you'll be WAGING (there's a word directly related to odds). It's difficult to be an eternal optimist and a realist too. It's imperative to be optimistic, but it's equally important to keep your feet on the ground and your eye on the ball by advancing your career with every opportunity.

Someone once said, "PLAN YOUR WORK, WORK YOUR PLAN." I suggest you take this advice and get yourself a weekly agenda. Each and every Monday morning, rise and shine to begin working your daily schedule. Follow up every contact you make, and exploit it to the fullest. You never know where or when that one lucky four-leaf clover will turn up.

When I first moved to Nashville, I heard countless success stories about such notables as Roger Miller, Willie Nelson, and Kris Kristofferson, among others. The stories were so glamorized that "making it" sounded like a slam-dunk. The success formula being that you needed only to become a little different and not let rejections bother you. Keep on keeping on, in other words. It wasn't until much later in my career that I learned that everybody just mentioned paid their dues and much, much more before they hit it big.

There was one relatively short success story of which I was a first-person eyewitness. It began one Saturday afternoon in the summer of 1969. I was killing time between an Opry Matinee and the evening's first show at a little bar called THE ACE OF CLUBS (long since defunct). A long haired lanky guy came up and sat down beside me and proceeded to tell me that he had just arrived in town and planned to make it big in the Music Business. He said he had just been released from prison up in Moundsville, West Virginia, and that a prominent Talent Agency Owner and Publisher had told him to come see him when he got out of jail. It seems the fellow had sent a bunch of tapes out from prison to Nashville of songs he had written while serving time. Somebody bit. He had a portable tape player with him and asked if I would like to hear a couple of his originals. I said, "why not?" As rough as the tape sounded, I sort of knew I was listening to something and somebody special.

I listened, complimented him and wished him the very best. He truly was one of the nicest strangers I had ever met. I must admit, I didn't tell him I had to leave to perform on the Grand Ole Opry that evening for fear he would want to tag along and go backstage. In those days, the Opry backstage was always so crowded you could barely get around. The show was then staged at the historic Ryman Auditorium, a much smaller facility than the present Opry House at Opryland USA.

It wasn't long – perhaps less than a year – before the young ex-prison inmate I had met by chance one summer afternoon was making a name for himself both as a songwriter and as a singer-performer. It wasn't long before he didn't need me or anyone else to get him backstage of any Country Music Show in the land. That young man was DAVID ALLEN COE. David did not have the career that perhaps he would have liked to have had, but nevertheless he hit fast, created a very unique fan following and sold a lot of records for Columbia (now Sony).

It always pays to look beneath the surface. That was a lesson I learned in the summer of 1969. By the way, David Allen Coe is absolutely nothing like the rough and tough biker image he portrays. Sorry if I've blown your cover, David.

I'm relating this story now because it's a positive example of a young man with all the ODDS against him exploiting the one contact he had made in Nashville from inside prison walls and finding a big FOUR-LEAF CLOVER. Odds are you won't be as lucky. But I won't bet against you even if I run into you at a little Nashville bar sometime, listen to your tape and really don't think much of it. In any case, I'll be sure to offer a word of encouragement and who knows, I might even ask you if you would like to visit backstage at the Grand Ole Opry (that is if they'll still let ME in).

CHAPTER TWENTY-ONE
I FEEL GREAT

Perhaps the most difficult of all professions in which to succeed are those requiring self-motivation. In that group, I think self-employed or employed sales people head the list of professionals who are challenged most. A great Sales Motivator once said that everyone in sales should get up bright and early, briskly walk to their bathroom, look in a mirror and exclaim, "I FEEL GREAT!" The idea being to get the day started on a "super high" positive note. I realize that rolling out of bed bright and early is hard enough for some of us without having to face ourselves in a mirror. The real point is that MIND CONDITIONING allows us to get a leg up on the day's challenges. You've got to THINK IT to DO IT. The glass has always got to be HALF FULL, not half empty.

I've had a special affection for the sales field since my early years in Broadcasting. As a "hotshot" News Director, I recall many heated discussions with our station's Sales Manager over whose job in the "BROADCASTING FOOD CHAIN" was most important. A couple of D.J.'s would always chime in, saying their roles were definitely THE most important. Our sales manager was female; highly unusual in those days. Her name was Cleo Johnston and she could hold her own in any discussion, heated or otherwise, male or female. Clee (as we called her) stopped us all cold one day during one of our MY JOB'S MORE IMPORTANT THAN YOURS forays. She said, "consider this, guys: nothing happens till somebody sells something" (this was the title of a popular sales book in the '60's).

When you give that premise some thought, there is nothing else left to discuss.

Later, when I became her boss as Station Manager, I had to approve our weekly payroll. When I saw her salary and commissions were more than three times what I was earning as her superior, I realized the wisdom of her words and gained an even greater respect for the sales profession. I already had plenty of respect for HER since she helped me land my first job in Broadcasting.

I've said all that to say this: SHOW BUSINESS *IS* THE SALES PROFESSION! The product is not a commercial on the radio. The product is YOU, YOUR PERSONALITY, YOUR TALENT and YOUR MUSIC! You face the same challenges as a Broadcast Time Sales Person, Insurance Agent or Car Sales Associate. They, too, must sell themselves before they can proceed to sell their respective product(s).

The greatest enemy of a Sales Professional is procrastination. Before you say anything HOSS, here's another oldie but goodie: DON'T PUT OFF TOMORROW WHAT YOU CAN DO TODAY. But wait, there's more: EVERYTHING COMETH TO HE WHO WAITETH…BUT THE ONE WHO EXCELS IS THE ONE WHO WORKETH WHILE HE WAITETH. (HOSS replies: "I'M ABOUT TO RALPH.")

The message is simple. Whether you're selling commercials, insurance, cars or your special talent on stage, you've got to give it a very large effort every day in order to become successful. The task is made easier if you truly love what you're doing. When you begin to see a few positive results and some fruit from some of your labor, you'll find yourself having the time of your life. At some point, you might even find yourself looking forward to the start of the next day. Who knows, one day you might even jump out of bed, run into the bathroom, look in your mirror and yell out, "I FEEL GREAT!"

CHAPTER TWENTY-TWO
SEDUCTIVE, ADDICTIVE and DESTRUCTIVE

If I had to single out just one of the many negatives of show business, it would have to be the countless pitfalls awaiting unsuspecting newcomers when they achieve enough success to begin traveling. Whether it's in support of a hit or a string of hit records, or whether an entertainer is just starting to make their mark in the small lounge/club circuit, life on the road takes its toll on everyone. Earlier, we touched on some of the problems which can arise, but there's much, much more to that story. A person unprepared for the so-called GOOD TIMES can easily ruin a career, but more importantly can just as easily ruin his life and the lives of those around him.

Life on "the road" seduces many, becomes an addiction to many others and has gone on to totally destroy still others. I speak from experience in this regard, though my life was not destroyed or even badly damaged. I saw first hand how late night partying with liquor and drugs, coupled with poor eating habits and lack of exercise, can send a person spiraling downward. Focus is easily lost, and upward mobility and effort become stagnated. I'm talking about normal people falling into this road trap, not just those with weak or addictive personalities. I feel the need to say that my motives here are to inform and educate not lecture.

It's always been my feeling that a person should never harp on a problem without offering some sort of workable solution. The solution I offer to the many problems evolving from roadwork can be served up with a single word: DISCIPLINE! If you're not already a disciplined person, work on becoming one – fast. The first step toward finding a disciplined path is to become an early riser. You can't "roar" all night if you know you've got to get up and pursue an active career agenda the next morning. Start a regular exercise program, such as walking or jogging. Learn to play golf, tennis or any other outdoor sport you can enjoy while away from home. Fill your day with healthy activities. Those activities will not only help keep you out of trouble, but you'll be amazed at the energy you'll develop for your nightly stage performances. Encourage your Personal Manager, Tour Manager, Booking Agent, or Record Company to schedule newspaper and broadcast interviews for you (and your group). If you're not far enough along to have any of those representatives just mentioned, schedule whatever sit-downs you can yourself. If you've never had a chart record, come up with interesting tidbits about yourself that would make a newsperson or Radio/TV personality want to talk with you. Local media reps are constantly on the look out for new and unusual human interest features. This is especially true in small or medium sized markets (cities). Just like New York, Los Angeles, Las Vegas or Miami, Nashville, Tennessee, is a magic name in entertainment circles. It's helpful to mention you're a Nashville-based act.

I'm not suggesting you become a boring workaholic. Not by any means. It's a fun business. Enjoy it, but as the saying goes, KNOW WHEN TO SAY WHEN. Or as a famous (disciplined) personality said to me around midnight at a pretty rowdy party a long time ago, "I'VE ENJOYED ABOUT ALL THIS I CAN STAND FOR ONE NIGHT." He left, but I couldn't. The party was in my hotel room. Actually, I had two parties in my room that night – THE FIRST and LAST! Lesson learned. Don't throw parties on the road. Attend them so you can choose when you want to leave.

When I said earlier that I speak from experience regarding personal problems road travel can cause, I would like to site THE specific instance when I made the determination that I was not living in a healthy situation. It occurred one night while sitting at a casino bar in San Juan, Puerto Rico. Some might say that I'd had a little too much to drink. I would say that I had merely been "over-served." Gone from home for nearly five-weeks (our group was performing an extended engagement on a cruise ship where every night is New Year's Eve); I was not a happy guy. Sometimes alcohol turns me into a big sentimental slob (it also makes you do funny things on tables in Mexican night clubs). HOSS, please don't tell everything you know about Mexico.

Anyway, back to the San Juan casino bar. I was feeling a little down – missing my wife and my life back in Nashville (if I recall correctly, you were also upset about being charged five dollars for a ten-ounce glass of beer). HOSS, in the words of former President Reagan, "THERE YOU GO AGAIN." Please put a sock in it!

For whatever reason, it occurred to me that the life I was leading at the time had seduced me. I had become addicted and if I continued, it would eventually destroy me. When I thought more about those three words (SEDUCTIVE, ADDICTIVE and DESTRUCTIVE) that were having such an impact on my very being, I realized by taking the first letter of each word, I could spell another word that summed up the entire thought – SAD.

Since that night in Puerto Rico, I try not to have such deep and disturbing thoughts. I also took some preventative action. We ceased accepting any extended engagements for longer than two-weeks. In addition, I make it a point to stay away from all casino bars in San Juan. However, I still frequent casino bars in Vegas. The beer there is free (glass or bottle) so long as you're playing video poker; but then that's another entirely different addiction. In most cases this one requires a twelve-step program to get under control.

CHAPTER TWENTY-THREE
NEED TURNS TO GREED
THEN BACK TO NEED

Having spent so much time performing in Las Vegas, Reno and Lake Tahoe, Nevada through the years, it's understandable that I would count a lot of casino personnel among some of the most interesting people I have ever met (I thought we just did the casino story). HOSS, PULLLEEEZE!

One very special former twenty-one dealer turned bookmaker used to keep me in stitches with his countless platitudes and profundities on gambling life. His name was Bill and he was always about three steps ahead of everybody when it came to having the right answers to just about any gambling question you could muster. When I met him, he worked in the Sports Book at the Desert Inn Hotel and Casino. This was after he had lost his wife, kids, home and car playing Blackjack (also known as 21). He said it was at that point, broke and homeless, that he realized he was gambling on the wrong side of the table. Over time, the house always wins. So he went to dealer school and began working his way back to prosperity. He quickly gained respect in the Vegas gambling community as a great "odds maker" (a person especially gifted with numbers who learns to determine odds FOR and AGAINST a gaming event or transaction). He had one of those unusual computer minds necessary to become successful in the gaming business.

Since both our roots stretched back to the Steubenville, Ohio, area, we hit it off immediately and became good friends. For most of you who are unaware, Steubenville was once known as "Little Chicago" and was a popular stop on the illegal gambling circuit. It became a hotbed for entertainers and gamblers who would later migrate west to Vegas and California. Steubenville native Dino Paul Crocetti (Dean Martin) was once a dealer at an after hours club there. Jimmy "The Greek" Snyder, famous Odds-Maker, Network Sports Broadcaster and Owner-Operator of a Public Relations firm in Vegas, was from Mingo Junction, Ohio (a little town 3-miles south of Steubenville). The late actor Robert Urich, who starred in the hit TV Series VEGAS, was born and raised one block from MY HOME PLACE in Toronto, Ohio, just 4-miles north of Steubenville.

Meanwhile, back to my Vegas buddy Bill and his quick wit. One afternoon, I dropped into the Desert Inn to see Bill and check the betting line on an Ohio State football game. Bill said that Ohio State was favored to win by three points. I said that USA Today has a better line, with Ohio State favored to win by two and a half. Bill, without giving it a thought, said, "well, call THEM and place your bet." Of course, USA Today does not take bets.

Another time, I was giving Bill some of the wealth of information I had stored up from reading the sports pages cover to cover that particular week. After about five-minutes of listening to me, Bill stopped me mid-sentence and asked, "DOES YOUR BODY EVER GET TIRED OF CARRYING YOUR HEAD AROUND WITH ALL THAT KNOWLEDGE IN IT?" Thinking back, Bill reminds me of a guy named HOSS, whom I would someday regretfully meet.

Bill was forever offering words of wisdom about the hazards of gambling. He once said, "NEED TURNS TO GREED, THEN BACK TO NEED." Those words are applicable to so many facets of life other than gambling. Take the Music Business, for example (that's right, Wellington...let's get back to the book).

During the '60's and '70's (and perhaps before), some of Country Music's biggest names began recording songs from their own Publishing Companies. Rather than search for genuine hit songs, some acts became greedy and capitalized on their fame and record selling ability by recording only songs from their own companies, many of which would be considered "average" at best. Had this been done on a limited basis, it would have been considered good business. There is certainly nothing wrong with a current "hit-maker" including a couple of his own songs or other songs in his Publishing Company in his latest album; an album which he knows is going to become a big seller. But greed consumed some acts, and many careers were damaged – some severely – by recording songs that were not quite the caliber of those on which their success was created.

Greed became such a dominant factor that some top recording acts required independent writers/publishers to surrender a portion of their ownership (copyright) of a song they planned to record before it ever got to the recording stage. Through the years, ownership (partial or otherwise) of many hit songs has contained the names of the artist singing them, even though the artist did not actually write or publish the material. It's been widely reported that Colonel Tom Parker (Elvis Presley's hard-nosed Manager) insisted on putting "The King's" name on many of the hits he recorded, demanding up to 50 percent of the writer's profits. Otis Blackwell, who wrote *DON'T BE CRUEL*, RETURN TO SENDER and many others is said to have gladly shared the bill with Elvis. It's even been reported that the Colonel himself appears as co-writer on some Elvis' records under an assumed name. All this is not to say that there are very few artists who can write, publish and record their own material. To the contrary, there are many. I merely point out the negatives of greed as a means for you to recognize various backroom deals you should be familiar with in the event your career begins to blossom. The practice is perfectly legal and in some cases very appealing to a new writer/publisher. A piece of something beats all of nothing.

Another clever business move popular in the '60's, '70's, '80's (and maybe even during the '90's and today) went something like this: a top act would strike a deal with another top act to feature each other's published music on their respective albums/CD's. The premise being that each act would record the other's song(s) on their next album or CD, and vice versa. Cool idea, huh? In my opinion, that is NOT greed, but rather simply good business; again, so long as the songs being swapped are top quality and "fit" the artist recording them.

If someday you find yourself at the top of the record charts and begin thinking of ways to enhance your already bulging bank account, try to remember the difference between good business and greed.

Remember the words of my friend "Vegas Bill" – NEED TURNS TO GREED THEN BACK TO NEED.

One more bit of wisdom that Bill passed along to me many years ago: he said if you insist upon betting on college or pro sports, bet small and for entertainment purposes only. Remember, as with Blackjack, Craps, Roulette and Poker, THE HOUSE ALWAYS WINS…and that's the name of *that* game!

CHAPTER TWENTY-FOUR
LISTEN and LEARN

Someone once said, "If you're talking, you're not learning." Aside from learning from your own mistakes (and from reading this book), the best way to catch on to the intricacies of show business is to find and hang out with those who have been in and around the Nashville Music Scene for a number of years. If you're lucky, you may even find someone who is willing to take you under their wing and serve as an honest to goodness mentor. That person doesn't always have to be a big-time Music Business success to provide you with the valuable knowledge you need to help you up the ladder. It's much easier to believe words of wisdom offered by someone who has already made it, but there are literally thousands of mildly successful music people in Nashville who truly know the ropes and are glad to be of help if approached properly.

Songwriters are a great source of Music Row info. Those, who have been on the Nashville scene for a period of time, have already lived through and learned from the same pitfalls we're trying to help you avoid. My first mentor was indeed a songwriter along with being a good country singer and a great entertainer. His name was and is Bill Brock. As an entertainer he was especially good in nightclubs where he could put forth his special brand of slightly off-color comedy.

When we met in the mid-'60's, Bill had been in Country Music for a number of years and had written a couple of big hits, namely: I'LL JUST HAVE A CUP OF COFFEE THEN I'LL GO (for Claude

King) and THERE'S A BLACK CLOUD HANGIN' OVER MY HEAD (for Leroy Van Dyke and Chubby Checker). His writer buddies included some of the best Nashville (and California) had to offer at the time. It's no secret that California has produced some great country talent over the years. Anyway, because of the hits he had written, Brock was also connected with Music City's top Label Heads and Producers.

Through daily meetings and social gatherings at his home, Bill gave me (and the other three Guys) the where-with-all to get a head start up the "Show-Biz" beanstalk. The course was NASHVILLE 101. Bill was one professor. Others followed. Some with more experience, some with far less. All helped to shave months and perhaps years off the usual Nashville learning curve.

It's important to note that I/we were good students. We hung on every word these veteran music men offered. When they talked, we listened. It didn't mean we were so naïve that we believed every word, but rather we gave all their information complete and total consideration as if it were the truth. Most of it was.

My experience in finding shortcuts is another example of the importance of networking. Contacts! Contacts! Contacts! You've got to get that big, thick music door open before you can get an opportunity to show your wares. Once the door opens, don't be like the guy who was standing at the airport when his SHIP finally came in. Be aggressive without being obnoxious. Be assertive without being arrogant. Whatever you do, treat your first big break as though you may never get another. Who knows, maybe you won't.

Your first major break into the recording field is probably THE most important; one which must be handled with care. Your initial reputation as an artist will surface when your temperament (or lack of it) in the recording studio is reported by those participating on your session(s). Your complete cooperation is a must. This is both the highest and lowest point of your young career. The highest in that you finally got a good record deal. The lowest in that you must bite your tongue at practically every decision made while in the studio. Your Producer, the Musicians he has hired and the Studio Engineer(s) are evaluating your every move. Talk about a network and/or pipeline of contacts. Even a minor display of attitude by a new artist will hit Music Row like a tornado the very next day, and it will probably be greatly exaggerated. On the other hand, this group of talented music people truly desires to give you high marks so don't do or say anything that will cause them to do otherwise. Once you've charted a hit or two, becoming a little more vocal is not only accepted but expected.

When it comes time for you to record your vocals (after instrumental tracks have been laid), chances are you will be in the studio with just your Producer and Studio Engineer(s). There is only one area in which I would ever dream of challenging a Producer: that is in the monumental task of *mixing*. If you have made a vocal mistake and wish to correct it on the spot, and you hear your producer say, "DON'T WORRY, WE'LL FIX IT IN THE MIX," do whatever it takes to get him to change his mind. Use all the tact you can find, but do not let the mistake go through with the hope it will be corrected later (perhaps weeks later) during the mixing process. Too many times, it never gets fixed. Why? Because if your producer has a FIX IT IN THE MIX attitude, he will oftentimes let several mistakes go by.

On our very first album (The Four Guys), I "popped a P" (which means I pronounced a word beginning with the letter "P" too harshly into the microphone) creating a popping sound. I pointed it out and was told not to worry we would fix it in the mix later. It got overlooked, and to this day (some thirty-years later), I cannot stand to hear that particular cut.

Any suggestion you might have in the recording studio should be directed to your Producer only and in private (not on mike). During your first session(s), my advice is to speak only when there is an obvious mistake and when no one is moving to correct it. This is an unlikely occurrence in the "big leagues," where an obvious mistake rarely gets overlooked.

For the most part, try to be contented to listen and learn. The studio will be the most important element in your career should you begin to find success in the Music Business. I'm not sure whether or not he coined the phrase, but the late George Morgan – Country Music Hall Of Fame and Grand Ole Opry Star - once told me that an act is only as big as his last record. He went on to say that whatever else you do in managing your career, by all means *stay focused on the recording phase*. That makes perfect sense to me. How 'bout you?

CHAPTER TWENTY-FIVE
FAME IS A FLEETING THING

How many times have you wished to be famous and adored by fans around the world? If you're like most of those trying to "make it," probably many times. But have you ever thought about what fame truly is and what you must do to hold onto it once you've achieved it? Probably not. A "smart butt" Grand Ole Opry staff musician once asked me how it felt to be a "fourth of an almost star" (referring to my one-fourth participation in The Four Guys). I proudly shot back that it was better than being no star at all (like him). I then thanked him for acknowledging that I was, in fact, a fourth of something on the rise and not the whole of something going nowhere.

You've heard people say, "be careful what you wish for." Speaking from experience gained through the eyes of a long career in Country Music, I have seen fame do marvelous things for many and become the root of all evil for others (money and fame are usually linked). Egos under control can accomplish great things for some, while others can run amuck and quickly crash and burn. My advice for those who are able to find stardom is to quickly place your feet on solid ground, save your money and live by the Golden Rule: "do unto others as you would have others do unto you" (I know what you're thinking HOSS, but don't say it). There are those who subscribe to another rule not quite so golden: IF YOU'VE GOT A BUDDY GOOD AND TRUE, SCREW YOUR BUDDY BEFORE HE SCREWS YOU. Sounds like a Wall Street way of life to me even though it has probably worked for many in THAT rat race over the years. The Music Business, however, is a *personality* business and requires many helping hands along the road to success.

If you plan to use your future stardom as a platform to advance your politics and personal views, it would be wise to already have your place in the Country Music Hall of Fame assured before taking such a gigantic leap of faith. Perhaps you should ask yourself early on exactly how you plan to treat your future fame. Would you prefer to possess a quiet type of fame and let your talent and music speak for you, or would you choose to continually stand atop a "soap box," pushing some political cause or candidate? One thing to remember the minute you announce your political affiliation or support for a particular candidate, you've automatically alienated about 50 percent of your potential fan base. At what point in your career does it make sense to lose half your potential following?

I wonder if The Dixie Chicks – probably the hottest group on the planet Earth early in 2003 – would have chosen a different path, if the option were available today, instead of trying to cater to a British audience's opposition to Gulf War 2. Lead singer Natalie Maines' adlib of saying she was ashamed that President George W. Bush was from "The Chicks" home-state of Texas cost the group considerable loss of record sales. More importantly, it caused a severe amount of damage to their image and popularity. Just prior to their remarks, the girls had been nominated for three major awards by The Academy of Country Music (the West Coast's version of The Country Music Association). The awards ceremony, held in Las Vegas and broadcast nationally, passed over The Dixie Chicks in all three nominated categories, their first total awards snub in several years.

There was a sign hanging in the control room of the Radio Station where I once worked which read: PLUG IN BRAIN BEFORE OPENING MOUTH! Perhaps "The Chicks" should have T-shirts made displaying those words instead of launching a low class (my opinion) campaign against fellow artist Toby Keith, who in support of the military had made some remarks against Natalie's comments in England.

As you may or may not recall, Maines wore a T-shirt with bold letters "FUTK" written on it during a TV satellite interview on awards night. Could the "TK" have referred to Toby Keith? Could the "FU" have meant what most everyone thought it meant? Equally to blame were some of Keith's fans who wore T-shirts with the letters "FUDC" on them. Could the last two letters have been a reference to Dixie Chicks? Could the first two once again mean exactly what most thought they meant? The entire demonstration dealt Country Music a severe blow in front of a national TV audience. There's an old proverb which suggests GREAT MINDS DISCUSS IDEAS; AVERAGE MINDS DISCUSS EVENTS; SMALL MINDS DISCUSS PEOPLE.

To add insult to injury, "The Chicks" failed to win any of the awards for which they were nominated and later said they were thinking of leaving Country Music altogether to concentrate on a career in The Pop Music Field. HUH? The Country Music Association membership must have taken note of those comments, since they nominated the girls in only one category for the fall, 2003 awards. They failed to win again. Coincidently, Toby Keith was nominated in several categories but did not win any awards. Perhaps the industry had heard enough petty bickering from all sides for the time being. However, the following spring, Toby Keith was nominated and won in four ACM awards categories, including: Entertainer of the Year, Male Vocalist of the Year, Album of the Year and Video of the Year, while The Dixie Chicks were not nominated in ANY category.

Only the years ahead will determine the amount of damage caused to one of the most popular acts in show business history. The off-cuff remark turned into an international controversy, together with a follow-up threat to leave the music genre, could have severe, long-term effects. Unlike Movie Stars and Rock 'N Roll Acts, Country Music Fans and their idols have an up close and personal relationship. The famous comic of the '20's and '30's, W.C. Fields, is said to have once remarked, "I DON'T CARE WHAT YOU SAY ABOUT ME, JUST SPELL MY NAME RIGHT," supporting the theory that there is no such thing as bad publicity. Believe me, in Country Music THERE IS such a thing as bad publicity, and its' affects can indeed be far reaching. Remember, the opposite of FAME is INFAMY (this is getting really heavy; please cool it with the EDITORIAL PAGE). HOSS, I've missed you lately, but not nearly enough!

CHAPTER TWENTY-SIX
UNCEREMONIOUS SUCCESS

It's a perfectly natural aspiration for anyone deciding to become a professional entertainer to reach for the stars. Anything less would show lack of desire, motivation and determination. But the old adage (used previously) that SUCCESS IS A JOURNEY, NOT A DESTINATION is exactly how young performers should evaluate their career progress.

I'm not suggesting you should initially begin letting yourself down easily in the event that you do not ultimately hit every goal you first set out to achieve. I am suggesting that you learn to take life's accomplishments to heart and be thankful for each and every one of them that comes your way. Remember, you're entering a career field that has a total success rate that falls somewhere just short of hitting the lottery. I say TOTAL SUCCESS meaning that you are striving to become the next Garth Brooks (FAT CHANCE!). HOSS, do you get a special kick out of raining on parades?

The Music Business, which on the surface appears to be unlike any other vocation IS exactly like other respectable professions. Yes, an F. Lee Bailey, Johnny Cochran or Perry Mason (Perry Mason?) only comes along every once in a while, but there are thousands of lawyers we've never heard of earning huge incomes and thoroughly enjoying their professional lives. The same scenario applies to the Music Business; especially the Country Music Business.

Room for great success is ever-present in the many phases mentioned earlier (i.e. Managing, Booking, Writing, Publishing, Producing, etc.).

But the opportunities available for both financial and personal rewards are also present on the *performer's* ladder as well. More times than I care to remember, I have wrongly opined regarding an entertainer's lack of success merely on the basis of their age, appearance, dress or length of time since their last hit record (OPINED? I'll bet you know lots of big words; SUBMARINE, for example). HOSS, have you ever considered haunting houses for a living?

Meanwhile, as one matures in the business, you learn that many of those who you once looked upon with great sympathy were in fact able to "buy and sell" large numbers of our current chart-toppers. It's the "DON'T JUDGE A BOOK BY IT'S COVER" thinking. From the musicians on stage to those on the rung just below the headliner, I have known numerous entertainers who have achieved UNCEREMONIOUS SUCCESS and who continue to succeed today on the strength of current and past reputations. Again, "hit records" are what it's about, but NOT what it's all about. Among other things, HITS are merely a gauge for the public's perception of success. Personally, I always gauged my success by how many and how my investments were doing. Yes, I must admit, a string of hits would have helped the process along much faster and to a much larger conclusion, but I'm pleased with MY JOURNEY.

Back to the subject of measuring the degree of success, it's been my experience that the top rung of the ladder is where we all aspire to be, but the "second or even third banana" spot is not so bad either. A supporting act gets an opportunity to steal the show every time the curtain goes up with no risk or blame if the show overall is not successful. Most of the pressure and responsibility lies with the person whose name is at the top of the marquee. Sure, both the personal and financial rewards are greater, but the weight of being on top is a lot to shoulder night after night, show after show. I'm not suggesting you shoot for second best because it's safer there, but rather if that's where you end up there are certainly far less comfortable places to be. Perhaps a better way to put it would be to say "always reach for the stars, but if you only get to the moon, you have still traveled a long way from home." The measure of that achievement can best be described as UNCERMONIOUS SUCCESS! Be proud of it!

CHAPTER TWENTY-SEVEN
PATIENCE OF AN OYSTER

We've all heard the phrase NO PAIN, NO GAIN. I once wrote a song containing the line: THEY SAY YOU'VE GOT TO HURT BEFORE YOU KNOW LOVE, AND IF THAT'S THE WAY IT GOES I KNOW IT ALL. Another original member of The Four Guys (Richard Garratt) wrote a song with a similar line: YOU'VE GOT TO KNOW THE SADNESS IN TEARS SO YOU'LL KNOW HOW TO SMILE.

These extreme emotions – PAIN to GAIN, HURT to know the JOY of LOVE, SADNESS to HAPPINESS – all really spell out what it takes to find an appreciative state of mind. There's a lot to be said for living the downside in order to fully appreciate the upside. Don't get excited; you won't have to plan on hitting bottom so you can enjoy the top when and if you ever get there. More than likely, you'll get to experience plenty of "hard times" quite naturally with no effort whatsoever. It's simply the nature of the "Music Business beast."

Again, I've said all this to say along with "appreciation," the operative word in your new music venture is PATIENCE. The late Country Music Legend, Faron Young – and I don't use the term "legend" loosely – told me early in my career that in order to find a safe haven (in your mind) while working in the entertainment business, you must develop the "Patience Of An Oyster." This is learned behavior and must be something you work on daily. There will be many times when you'll want to throw in the towel and head for home. Pride will help you in the beginning, since no one wants to return home a failure. But later on, you'll have to learn how to "hang in there" on your own and find – I should say MAKE - positive things happen to advance your career effort. Once again, all this applies only if you learn for sure and for certain that you truly do have something to offer in the way of talent and ability.

Many Nashville greats learned to develop strong stage personalities in order to keep their confidence level at its peak. They learned to think early on that there was no obstacle or audience they couldn't overcome and conquer; "win over" over might be a better way to put it. (See HOSS, I didn't need you on that one.)

The late Marty Robbins was known for his super-confident approach to stage work. Some would say he was downright cocky when the curtain went up. Backstage, though, he appeared standoffish, with little to say to anyone. Many of his peers (but not those who truly knew him) thought he was unsociable and not a nice person to be around. In the beginning, I was one of those who kept his distance from Super Star Marty until I got an opportunity to work a few road engagements with him. It was only then that I saw him for what he really was – SHY. That's an observation I have carried with me through the years and have found it to hold true of most people – in and out of show business – who initially come on a little too strong. More often than not, those who exhibit an overwhelming, even abrasive, personality are merely covering up a shy inner self; something like a superiority complex covering up an inferiority complex.

I have another mildly successful friend who takes the whole confidence route a little too far. He has a plaque on his dressing room wall which reads: "IT'S HARD TO BE HUMBLE WHEN YOU'RE AS GREAT AS I AM." As always, somewhere between obnoxious and humble is the best place to be.

Personally, I try to live my life attempting to adhere to the words of a great man AND to the philosophy of a simple prayer. The great man was millionaire philanthropist Robert Woodruff, who turned Coca Cola from a drug store novelty to a soft drink known around the world. He is quoted as saying, "THERE IS NO LIMIT TO WHAT A MAN CAN DO OR WHERE HE CAN GO IF HE DOESN'T

MIND WHO GETS THE CREDIT." The Serenity Prayer has had the greatest impact on my life long before I knew it was the anthem of Alcoholics Anonymous. For those of you who are unaware, it reads: "GOD, GRANT ME THE ABILITY TO CHANGE THE THINGS I CAN, ACCEPT THE THINGS I CANNOT CHANGE, AND THE WISDOM TO KNOW THE DIFFERENCE." Acquiring the "Patience of an Oyster" can also be helpful.

CHAPTER TWENTY-EIGHT
EARTH – IT'S A BIG PLANET

I remember asking Charley Pride, during one of our many national tours, where he planned to perform when his U.S. draw power began to wane. He said without hesitation, "IT'S A BIG PLANET." That comment opened my mind to endless possibilities and exposed my thinking to an international school of thought.

Just in case you're not ready to stop performing when your career says you should begin thinking about it, imagine what an overseas tour would do for your entire organization. Country Music continues to grow in popularity throughout Europe, Australia and Asia. The Netherlands has been a "hotbed" for Country Entertainers for decades.

The key is to start laying ground work early in your career by making sure your recordings are distributed world-wide. Connect with overseas Talent Promoters and perhaps plan to attend some of the big Music Festivals. First tours – for relative newcomers – yield small amounts of revenue, but the exposure and record sales are usually enhanced greatly. Keep one thing in mind: overseas audiences enjoy traditional Country Music and show great appreciation for Fringe, Rhinestones, Cowboy Hats, Boots, etc. Don't go too far uptown with your stage presentation (music or dress). I've known major acts that were "booed" off stage for trying to be something other than what the European or Asian concert-goer came to see.

Overseas audiences seem to be much more appreciative than those here at home. I guess it's because they are not so "entertainment spoiled." Even as close as our neighbor to the north (Canada), it becomes evident that Country Music acts are treated with greater respect and admiration.

I recall a Charley Pride Tour which took us from one Canadian coast to the other playing the beautiful Queen Elizabeth Theatre circuit all along the way. Sellout crowds and repeated standing ovations became the norm night after night. The Canadian part of the tour concluded in Vancouver, British Columbia, on the West Coast; again, sold out with several curtain calls. The very next night, we played a major arena in nearby Seattle, Washington, USA, to an audience about half the size and to a less than enthusiastic response. Same show; same music; same presentation as the night before, but a very different result. Talk about bursting a bubble. A band member jokingly remarked, "GOD IT'S GREAT TO BE HOME – 'A'?"

Becoming an International Star is a great way to go if you can pull it off. Acts like the late Roy Orbison made touring Europe an annual event when his U.S. Star began to fade. Though as popular as ever in the United States at career end, overseas concerts kept his name in lights throughout his life.

Grand Ole Opry member George Hamilton IV has also made performing internationally his career path for decades. Billie Jo Spears, a Country Star in the '60's and '70's, became an even bigger marquee draw abroad for many years after her U.S. record sales began to taper.

There are numerous other entertainers who have had considerable success and lengthened their careers by cultivating the overseas markets. It's well worth the effort and insures you the option of never running out of stages to play. Charley Pride was soooo right in his observation that EARTH IS INDEED A BIG PLANET, and entertaining is just as much fun in London as it is in Dallas. In fact, it just might be a curtain call or two better!

CHAPTER TWENTY-NINE
I WISH I HADN'T SAID THAT

One of the most difficult areas of stage work to master is the art – and it is an art – of verbal communication. Having made my living in Broadcasting prior to entering the Music Business, I had a leg up on most trying to verbalize their way through a stage performance. I'm talking about all those times – beginning with your initial hello – between songs, skits or bits where it is imperative to build a stage personality and get your audience into your overall performance. Your singing and your music comprise the cake; your banter, sense of humor and actions add the icing.

There are very few acts able to succeed on stage without communicating with their audience in ways other than their music. The strong, silent types like Alan Jackson and George Strait; the cool, sexy personas, such as the late Conway Twitty and Marty Robbins; or the charismatic personalities of Charley Pride and Merle Haggard were/are among the few able to pull off a successful show with very little stage banter. Everyone else, for the most part, had better develop an act and start coming up with some clever things to say. Notice I say clever, not stupid or immature.

How do you develop an act? It starts with the basics of memorizing a skeletal routine that allows you to create a personable initial greeting, then pace your show with fast and slow songs and informative, interesting and even humorous introductions. It's not necessary to introduce every song unless there is something specific that the audience should know about a particular number. When and if the time ever comes that you are able to sing your own hits, the stage chatter can be kept to a minimum. Conway Twitty had built such a library of hits that ultimately his only spoken words on stage were "HELLO DARLIN', NICE TO SEE YOU," which was the first line of one of his biggest hits. However, until that day occurs (if ever) get the CHIT CHAT moving, but always know what you're going to say before you say it.

There are times when something spontaneous occurs on stage or in the audience that brings unexpected response or laughter from the rafters. When these times occur, you have the beginnings of your own act. In other words, be sure to incorporate that entertaining event into your next night's performance. You'll also, from time to time, come up with a funny adlib while telling the audience a story or introducing band members. If it gets audience response, leave it in (as we say). It takes time, but the more and better you communicate, the more fun you and your audience will have and the faster your act will evolve.

While your act is in the development stages, there are other ways to keep the audience interested in your presentation. This assumes they like your singing and your music. Don't be afraid to smile and show off those "pearly whites." Be sure to make as much individual eye contact as possible. Sometimes stage lights are so bright that it's hard to see past the first few rows, but even though you can't see *them*, always remember they can see *you*.

A lot of entertainers are reluctant to look their audience members in the eyes. In fact, many look out *over* the audience. Some say they try to imagine the crowd is naked in order to keep a pleasant look on their faces. If that works for you, go for it...the naked part that is.

The more you practice eye contact, the more enjoyable your work will become and the more your audience will enjoy you. Look at it this way, if you have nothing to say or do and are merely letting your singing do all the work, what incentive does anyone have to buy a ticket or pay an entertainment charge? They may as well stay home and put on one of your CD's. They come to see you in person because it's up close and personal. On stage, you're no longer just a voice on their radio or stereo.

Those who develop and master strong stage/TV personalities usually have long-lasting careers. Veteran acts such as Jimmy Dean, Johnny Cash, Barbara Mandrell, Ferlin Husky, Brenda Lee and The Statler Brothers are but a few of the many Country Entertainers who consistently wowed audiences with great entertainment along with their recorded hits. Among the newer country performers who have learned how to work a stage and a crowd, I especially enjoy Martina McBride, Tim McGraw, Billy Ray Cyrus, Reba McIntyre and of course, Garth Brooks. Without big hit records, our group (The Four Guys) learned early on we had better become entertainers first and hope for hits later if we were to survive. That thinking served us well for more than three decades.

One of the best ways to make your stage dialogue appealing is to develop continuity and smooth segues between something that has just happened and the introduction of the next song, person, bit or skit. For example, you've just finished your version of the gospel anthem *AMAZING GRACE*, which concludes the main body of your show. You are just about to thank the band for their performance and introduce them individually before presenting your big show closer. You might say something like: WHAT A GREAT OLD SONG, AMAZING GRACE. WE'VE GOT A PRETTY AMAZING BAND BACK HERE WHO WE THINK HAS DONE AN AMAZING JOB TONIGHT. JOIN US IN GIVING THEM A GREAT BIG HAND, etc. Smooth transitions will give your show a polished look and feel and thereby help you to become a better entertainer.

A good lawyer knows the answer in advance to any question he/she asks of a witness. A good stage spokesperson will always know what he or she is going to say before saying it (Wellington, you're repeating yourself; you said that earlier). HOSS, why don't you go fuel up the bus and practice going out of town?

Sometimes, even when you know what you're going to say, things won't come out exactly like you had planned to say them. One night while hosting a Grand Ole Opry segment, I was to present two other acts for a couple of songs each, as was the usual Opry format. The first act was a young performer who had just scored her second top ten hit record. It was her first time as a guest on The Opry. My introduction of this very attractive young lady went something like this: "Ladies and Gentlemen, it's always a lot of fun to host portions of our Opry shows, because most generally we get an opportunity to present entertainers with a lot of talent and oftentimes a lot of beauty. I want to present a young lady now who certainly has a little bit of each…a little bit of talent (this is where I began to realize I had just stepped in it) and a little bit of (there's no turning back now) BEAUTY! Give her a big hand, Miss So and So." She stormed on stage, grabbed the mike from my hand and if looks could kill, I most certainly would have been one dead "quarter of an almost star." Keith Bilbry, one of the Opry Staff Announcers, was quick to remind me after the show that The Opry is broadcast on WSM – 50-thousand watts of clear channel radio and is heard practically everywhere in North America. He added, "and by the way Sam, tonight's IN-HOUSE ATTENDANCE IS CAPACITY – 4,400." Talk about rubbing salt in the wound.

By no means was this the only time I ever stuck my foot in my mouth on The Opry stage or on other stages, but it was certainly one of the most embarrassing moments of my life. If you should be lucky enough to enjoy a long career, there are sure to be many times that what you meant to say and what you actually say will be poles apart. Stay alert, and think and speak slowly or you, too, will have lots of opportunities to say, "I WISH I HADN'T SAID THAT."

CHAPTER THIRTY
REMEMBER TO DANCE WITH
THE ONE THAT BRUNG YA!

The first time I ever heard that remark was when Roy Acuff softly scolded The Four Guys upon our return to The Opry after a two-month absence caused by a long road tour with Hank Williams, Jr. I remember "The King" lecturing us on The Opry's importance to our careers and that we needed to forever give back and participate in as many Opry Shows as possible. Once upon a time an Opry member was required to perform on at least twenty-six Saturday night Opry shows annually. In the old days, Fridays and Saturdays were prime work nights on the road, where the earning power was many times greater than The Opry. Once a certain degree of fame was achieved, many acts surrendered their Opry Membership in order to increase their earnings. Consequently, the required performance number of twenty-six shows was later lowered to twenty, then to twelve. Eventually, half credits were given for matinees and Friday nights, The Opry's way of making it much easier for a member to full-fill their Opry commitment. But just fulfilling the commitment was not good enough for Mr. Acuff and a select number of acts which he felt were extremely important to the Opry's stage presentation. I'm proud to say that he placed us in that special group of Opry performers.

You see, Roy Acuff was an entertainer first and foremost. The Opry is a live radio stage show. Yes, there are commercials to work around and yes, there was a vast radio audience that couldn't see the countless antics going on during the show; but Mr. Acuff was aware of all the elements involved – the radio listeners and the in-house audience. He had numerous entertaining skits for both, but he especially liked to come up with new and different ways of catering exclusively to those who had driven hundreds of miles and PAID to see a live Opry Show. Among his entertainment tricks were dozens of difficult stunts with a Yo-Yo and the balancing of his fiddle and bow on his chin and forehead. All the members of his band – The Smokey Mountain Boys – were showmen as well; most notably the late "Bashful Brother Oswald," who had been with "The King" from the beginning of his career. In later years, after Mr. Acuff's passing, The Opry awarded full membership status to Oswald, whose real name was Pete Kirby.

Roy Acuff truly loved The Opry and its legions of fans world-wide. He instilled his loyalty toward this great American institution in those he took the time to mentor. He was a man of his word in every way. If he said, "the sun will shine tomorrow," better dig out your shades.

The point of all this (ah, at last) is to never forget your roots; never get "above your raisin's" and always remember those who helped you when you needed it most. If you ever become successful in the music world, you can thank your mentors and those who bought your records or came to see you in person – YOUR FANS. Giving back to them takes so very little effort; something as small as a kind smile, hand-shake or autograph. Minnie Pearl once said while encouraging a young performer prior to her first Opry show, "Honey, just go out there and love 'em and they'll love you right back."

Roy Acuff opened every show with the sound of a train whistle leading into one of his biggest hits, WABASH CANNONBALL. Minnie Pearl opened every show with her patented line, "HOWDY, I'M JUST SO PROUD TO BE HERE." Most every successful act will spotlight or otherwise feature their signature hit or pay tribute to the thing that brought them to prominence. Whether it's was an astute Talent Scout, a Hit Record, a Catch Phrase or a Great Institution such as The Grand Ole Opry, always REMEMBER TO DANCE WITH THE ONE(S) THAT BRUNG YA!

CHAPTER THIRTY-ONE
CREATIVE CONTROL

We have discussed throughout this presentation the need to listen to the pros – assuming you've found some or assuming some have found you – and let them guide your career in a steady upward direction. This is especially important in the early days of your rise to prominence (remember the chapter LISTEN and LEARN?) There comes a time when you begin to acquire the business knowledge being taught and you will start making many career decisions on your own. In fact, you will begin to clash with certain members of your team regarding actions being taken on your behalf; particularly those decisions made without your knowledge or approval.

Regardless of the power you surrendered to your Management Team in that first big management contract (chances are you surrendered plenty), a good Personal Manager who is truly in it for the long haul will make it a point to discuss and seek your approval of any and all major decisions to be made. As your career begins to gain momentum, your opinion will suddenly be taken more seriously. Why would the same thoughts and ideas you had as a "NOBODY" all of a sudden become "JUST THE RIGHT THING TO DO"? BECAUSE JUST AS SUCCESS BREEDS ACCEPTANCE, IT ALSO BREEDS RESPECT.

In the early days of his career, I booked Larry Gatlin into The Four Guy's Harmony House for a week long engagement. He sat on a stool by himself and played mostly songs he had written. He drew so well that I re-booked him and paid extra for him to bring along some family members for accompaniment, including brothers Rudy and Steve. This too was a successful engagement. Larry was always very gracious contrary to what some in "the Nashville rumor mill" have said. From time to time he would stop by the Harmony House just to visit after he became a major star attraction.

I recall one evening we were all sitting around our dressing room listening to some of Larry's latest original material. He played one particular song and asked how we liked it. I, very enthusiastically, said "MAN THAT'S A HIT." He said, "OH REALLY? I PLAYED IT FOR YOU A YEAR AGO IN THIS SAME ROOM and YOU DIDN'T THINK MUCH OF IT." TOUCHÉ! SUCCESS BREEDS RESPECT.

When and if you begin to acquire it, there is a fine line as to when and how much you should assert your "clout." I've seen too many acts start down a path of self-destruction with a "know-it-all" attitude after only a limited amount of success. One act in particular refused to listen to his advisors and mentors after solid accomplishments on a major label. His initial five-year recording contract was about to expire; he had charted several hits, so the label had prepared a generous five-year renewal. Not good enough for our new self-proclaimed Super Star. He took the contract, scratched out most of the label's stipulations and wrote in his own. These reportedly included a new tour bus and a half-million-dollar signing bonus – considered outlandish demands in the late '70's and early '80's. He then returned the contract renewal and reportedly NEVER heard from the major label again. Other than a failed album that was later released on a small label, his budding recording career died on the vine.

It's important for you to maintain "creative control" of your career without becoming a "control freak." If you're like most entertainers, your greatest input and importance will lie in decisions being made from the front of the stage to the rear. That means the organization and staging of your show and all that goes into it. At the same time, don't ever believe that just because your PM, Booking Agent, Publicist or even Stage Hands don't sing, dance or play an instrument that they are incapable of a good idea as it pertains to your stage presentation. Listen to everybody in your organization and give consideration or even implementation to a thought or suggestion offered in the interest of improvement. Keep that ego in check and don't think all ideas are bad just because they didn't come from you.

The ability to maintain a certain degree of creative control should be a major point of contention with you even as you consider the terms and agreements of your first Personal Management and Recording Contracts. During those early contract negotiations, you must demonstrate the willingness to be flexible. At the same time, don't be afraid to stand tall when it comes to providing your input with regards to material to be recorded along with the ways and means of presenting IT and YOU to the public. You'll have to concede plenty in all other areas of contract negotiations and concede you should…willingly. Always remember exactly where you are on the "Show-Biz" ladder (for real, not imagined) and you'll make the right decisions.

I should also say that even when you're "standing tall," do so with grace, sincerity, tact and always with a touch of class. You know…be smart like a HOSS, er, uh… I mean like a fox.

CHAPTER THIRTY-TWO
THEY'RE PAYING ME
TO DO THIS?

If you're already fronting or otherwise participating in a small club performing group, you no doubt have said these words when you received your first paycheck, "I CAN'T BELIEVE THEY'RE ACTUALLY PAYING ME TO DO THIS;" especially when you've gladly done it (performing) hundreds of times for nothing. That special love of music and the desire (and need) to get up in front of people we all have during the early years is impossible to explain to friends and relatives – parents in particular. Moms and Dads the world over have lectured their children by saying, "DO YOU WANT TO BE IN SHOW BUSINESS OR DO YOU WANT TO GET A REAL JOB?" I'm happy to say my parents were not among those who tried to discourage me from a singing, broadcasting or show-business career. Hard working and of average means, my folks were locked into an environment whereby their choices for the future were limited. I think they were encouraged that maybe I wanted to venture out and see what the rest of the world had in store. Don't get me wrong. My parents were devoted to each other and were very happy with their small-town lifestyle. They both had lots of friends and plenty of things to enrich their lives, including a three week fishing vacation once a year in Canada. Those trips – many of which I took with them – were certainly some of the fondest memories of my young life. I just think, like most parents, they hoped I would do more and have an even better life than they had enjoyed. During those early years dealing with a tough job market after my discharge from the Navy and the rough going after my move to Nashville, I was forced to call on their support more than once. They never failed me and I've never forgotten, though both have long since passed on.

Those many sacrifices we all must make in order to get a foothold in the music industry can become special moments in our lives and should always be remembered. They can be called upon whenever we become a little too jaded or unappreciative of what we have accomplished, no matter the level of achievement. The fact that you're trying at all and doing what most of your peers either can't do or wouldn't have the nerve to do is plenty of reason to feel good about yourself and your efforts.

I have known a rather large group of one time successful recording acts who have apparently forgotten where they came from and what they have accomplished. Mostly older entertainers, they have grown bitter because their time at the top of the charts has passed and they feel the Music Business has cast them aside for the new breed of Country Artists. Most did not make the large amounts of money in their "hay-day" as today's successful recording stars. Most, unfortunately, did not or could not squirrel away sufficient money in their peak earning years to enjoy their twilight time. Many are still scrambling for personal appearances and willing to take anything that comes their way for pitifully low wages.

The recurring theme for many of these veteran performers is, "WE GAVE THEM THE BEST YEARS OF OUR LIVES AND NOW THEY DON'T WANT US ANYMORE." I'm sympathetic to their plight − to a point. My true thoughts, which I've expressed to many of them face to face, are yes, you gave them the best years of your lives, but they gave you the opportunity of a lifetime and paid you handsomely (at the time). There's no blame to be laid anywhere except in your own organizational camp.

The lesson here for someone desirous of "Show-Biz" stardom is make as many correct choices as possible along the way and save the dough you're making while you're rolling in it (when and if it comes your way). In order to retain a pleasant attitude in your golden years when "the ride" is finally over, I recommend we all look back to when we first said, "I CAN'T BELIEVE THEY'RE ACTUALLY PAYING ME TO DO THIS."

CHAPTER THIRTY-THREE
LEND A HAND – TOUCH
A HEART

No, this is not a chapter supporting the United Way or some other charity. This is a subject that deals with suggestions for you should you become that "one in a million" person to jump through all the right hoops and succeed in the Music Business. Suggestions dear to my soul and from which I have greatly benefited, as a receiver and a giver.

Once again, let's assume you have gotten off the launch pad and are enjoying a small amount of music success. The minute you see some career progress, you should begin to think of ways and means to help others just starting out. Any little piece of experience you gain (good or bad) can become extremely valuable to a complete and total novice. It also helps you – acting in a mentor role– to etch those experiences in your own psyche to be called upon whenever needed in the future.

In the big cities they call it gaining STREET SMARTS; in Show Business its building maturity and acquiring entertainment savvy. In any case, your limited amount of time and effort in Nashville will continue to build your knowledge base and make some of your more important decisions much easier. Remember, experience creates knowledge and awareness; both necessary tools to grow and achieve.

No matter how far you are able to climb up the music ladder, I promise someone will have helped you every step of the way. Perhaps their motivation was not entirely for your benefit and perhaps they benefited as much or more than you, but nonetheless, you will have gotten a helping hand when you needed it. "Please" and "Thank you" goes a long way in life; both in and out of business. Never forget those who helped you, and pass it on whenever you can to those who follow.

Fortunately, the Country Music Business is a friendly home in which to reside. As I've said from the beginning of this work, music people in Nashville will not only help those on the rise, but will do so willingly. This is especially true if they think you have the necessary qualities to "make it." I can cite example after example of music insiders and outsiders who gladly gave their time – and in some cases money – to move my/our career forward. I particularly recall the assistance given by a recording studio engineer who later became a studio owner. His name was Johnny Scoggins and his help came at a time early on when we sorely needed studio experience and product in order to obtain a major label recording contract. Johnny was a laidback, patient and extremely knowledgeable studio person who knew the ways of Nashville inside-out. He worked with our Writer-Manager Bill Brock to allow us lots of inexpensive studio time in order to experiment and record several original songs one of our group members, Richard Garratt, had put together. One of the songs was called *SOMEWHERE-NOWHERE* and was heavily considered by at least two of the city's most prominent record labels. It was later turned down by both labels but just being considered gave us the morale boost we desperately needed at that time.

A couple of years later when Johnny had become very successful in the studio business, he approached our group about putting together a series of sessions to re-record SOMEWHERE-NOWHERE and three other original songs written by yours truly and fellow members Garratt and Brent Burkett. This time, the recording budget was expanded greatly. In fact, there was a full orchestra – complete with large horn and string sections – to enhance the independent venture. The songs and arrangements were not very "country sounding" but rather more along the lines of the type of hit records Glen Campbell was having at the time (i.e. BY THE TIME I GET TO PHOENIX, GALVESTON and WICHITA LINEMAN). Perhaps recording mellow, well-orchestrated material in a then "gut-bucket, Country Music recording town" was not the wisest choice we could have made in 1969. However, the sessions were pitched to Mercury Records; they liked what they heard and we landed our first major label recording contract, all because of the helping hand of one Johnny Scoggins.

Here is the beauty of the Music Business: once good things start to happen in your career, a force called MOMENTUM comes into play, causing more good things to happen. The trick for you to learn – and learn fast – is to do everything in your power to keep "OLE' MO" in your corner and help him whenever and wherever you can. This is the time when you really need to ratchet up your drive and creativity to keep this positive force moving forward. This is when you really need to start kicking butts and taking names (figuratively speaking, of course).

Just like the Jerry Reed oldie says, "WHEN YOU'RE HOT, YOU'RE HOT, WHEN YOU'RE NOT, YOU'RE NOT." If you're lucky enough to reach the "hot property status," keep in mind it's not an endless winning roll of the dice. In the old days, a successful Country Music career could last fifteen to twenty years and longer. Today, with some exceptions, you're lucky to be on top for longer than five-years. Three to five years or less is about average these days. When you consider those figures, new meaning is given to the phrase, STRIKE WHILE THE IRON IS HOT.

Whatever degree of success you manage to achieve, do yourself and your business a favor by remembering those who helped you, and do the same for others. "LEND A HAND – TOUCH A HEART" is not only the right thing to do, but it makes you feel good too. Remember the words of BESSIE THE COW (if she could talk): "on a cold Wisconsin morning, A WARM HAND IS ALWAYS APPRECIATED" (I thought HEE-HAW was cancelled).

CHAPTER THIRTY-FOUR
YOU GOTTA HAVE HEART

I decided to include a wonderful human-interest story here about a young man and his desire and love for the Music Business. Much can be learned from those who are willing to do anything and everything in order to improve their worth and value just to become a part of the wild and crazy world of entertainment.

When things start to get a little rough in your career climb, I promise the following story will serve you in positive ways never imagined.

Throughout this writing, I have mentioned The Four Guy's venture into the theatre-restaurant business with a Nashville venue called THE HARMONY HOUSE. This was an enterprise created and operated by "The Guys" as a means to provide a home base for themselves and a way to maintain the year around services of a professional musical back-up unit – also known as a band (you don't leave anything to the reader's imagination do you?). HOSS, I'm glad you're back. When can we celebrate your next leave of absence?

Anyway, I want to pass along my thoughts about one of the of more than fifty music and restaurant personnel we employed. This is about a young man who became THE MOST UNFORGETTABLE AND COLORFUL CHARACTER I ever met. This is the TRUE story of "THE MUNCHKIN."

He was just a kid when I met him, a little over 18. That was the winter of 1975. His name was Donnie Maloney and he was the oldest of four boys; the younger three of whom were super students and destined for big things academically in college with promising careers assured thereafter. Donnie came from exceptionally "good stock," the son of Don and Harriet Maloney of Brentwood, Tennessee (an upscale Nashville suburb). Both his father and grandfather headed up large, successful accounting firms.

Donnie, though graduating from one of the area's best private schools, found that he and higher education just didn't hit it off very well. He had tried a semester at The University of Tennessee, but decided that college life was not for him. Though he didn't sing or play a musical instrument, he was a born "ham" and loved music and entertainment. His uncle, Buddy Wilkins, was in charge of the Lighting Department for Opryland Productions at Opryland USA in Nashville. I think this is how and where Donnie caught the "Show-Biz" bug.

He heard The Four Guys had just opened a supper club and were featuring a Vegas-style show with elaborate sound and lighting systems. Though his only experience was his connection with his uncle at Opryland, Donnie applied for the job of sound and light man.

I'll never forget the day he came to the Harmony House to apply for the job. Fresh out of "Big-Orange Country" (U.T.-Knoxville), Donnie walked in wearing orange and white gym shorts, a University of Tennessee football jersey, orange and white tennis shoes and the biggest white Hoss Cartwright (different Hoss, HOSS) cowboy hat I had ever seen. When I questioned him on his unusual appearance, he said he had heard sound and light guys were considered kinda strange and colorful and he wanted to look the part when applying for this job. I explained to him that this was not just a sound and light job and that it required someone who didn't mind wearing several hats. He said, "how about just one big hat?" And so he was hired; officially as our sound and light man, but also as an errand runner and valet for the group. He later would help out as a chauffeur for our kids, taking them to special events when we couldn't be there. Eventually, he became our Concessionaire and Road Manager.

Donnie loved comedy and had visions of becoming a stand-up comic. In fact he (with my help) developed a comedy routine that was to become a very important seven minutes of our club act. He became the very best at whatever duties he was given to perform.

Donnie had health problems from early childhood (mostly kidney-related). He battled for his life many times. In fact, he often referred to himself as a "walking miracle." Due to his condition, he didn't grow very tall, prompting our drummer, Johnnie Barber, to affectionately refer to him as "The Munchkin." Soon thereafter, he became "Munch" to us all.

Munch loved to laugh and loved to make others laugh. He became our very best audience night after night all by himself. During our nightly shows, he would sit in the sound and light booth, run the equipment and laugh at the top of his lungs at every line or gesture on stage. He would laugh as though he had never heard the routines before, and laugh so hard and loud that soon the entire audience would begin to laugh with him. Consequently, we would receive far greater audience response than we had actually earned; sort of priming the well.

Everybody who ever knew Munch has a bag full of tales to tell about him. Here are but a few of mine: One afternoon after he began working at The Harmony House, I gave him $20.00 to mow the lawn around the building and parking lot. Later that day, I went outside to check on his progress, only to find two neighborhood kids running the lawn mower and Munch sitting under a shade tree sipping a cool drink. He had paid the kids $5.00 each while he pocketed $10.00 for supervising the job. Right away, I saw an entrepreneur in the making.

During our first year at The Harmony House, we tried to come up with as many ways possible to market our new club venture. Along with the usual amount of newspaper, radio and local magazine advertising, we had quite a bit of success with handbills, or flyers. One of Munch's many duties was to circulate around the Country Music Hall of Fame and Music Row (where tourists and tour buses gathered) and pass out flyers to anyone who would accept them. He would do that and much more. For example, he would sneak onto tour buses while tour groups were inside the Hall of Fame and lay a flyer on every seat. If he was driving down any street in Nashville and saw a tour bus pulled over for any reason, he would stop, strike up a conversation with the Bus Driver and pass out those flyers to anyone on or near the bus.

The little sports car he drove in those days was always packed with flyers in both the trunk and backseat. One night on his way to work, he had a collision with another car (not his fault). He called to say he would be late for our show; that he had been in an accident but that he was not hurt nor was anyone else. I asked him what he was doing at that minute. He said, "I got a great crowd gathered around these banged-up cars, so I'm passing out lots of flyers." It was shortly after the accident that he bought the first of his many white corvettes. For a while, he bought and sold them like a professional used car dealer.

Munch desperately wanted to learn how to drive our big Silver Eagle tour bus. He felt that the more he knew about all phases of Show Business, the more secure he would be in it. One night, without my knowledge or permission, one of our group members gave him the driving lessons he wanted. For obvious reasons, I was not supportive of him driving a big bus, ours or anyone else's. He learned secretly and practiced for weeks late at night after closing. He came to me one morning and said, "Pops," (which is what he called me) "what say I drive the bus on our next road trip?" Astonished by the question, I replied, "You drive a bus?" "Can you drive a bus?" He said, "I'm tellin' you what's the truth. I can put her where you can't shine a light." Well, with much reservation, we tried him out as a Bus Driver. Guess what? He was one of the smoothest driving bus drivers we ever had.

Speaking of the bus and road trips, Munch got to know the habits (good and bad) of traveling musicians. He learned that many of them fail to plan very far ahead before embarking on a long road trip. We would always make a fuel stop before leaving town, patronizing one of the local truck stops. This would be the time to load up on cold drinks and snacks, since the bus would have a travel range of about 500-miles and would not be stopping anytime soon. Then, at about 1:00 A.M., while motoring down some long, lonesome highway and knowing everyone could use a nice snack, Munch would loudly announce, "O.K. BOYS, MUNCH'S MARKET IS NOW OPEN FOR BUSINESS." Out would come a vast assortment of snacks which he would sell to everyone for about three times what he had paid for them. Munch's Market was indeed a huge success.

While selling our albums and tapes after shows at The Harmony House (we didn't have CD's in those days), Munch would chant various attention-getting lines about our recorded product. One of his favorite was, "Four Guy's albums, three for $10.00, Four Guy's tapes, three for $15.00, or take The Four Guys home with you; ALL FOUR for $20.00!"

Then there was the night when Munch surprised me on stage during the middle of our show. He announced that he was turning in his notice and returning to his previously successful profession of "LUMBERJACKIN." I said, "LUMBERJACKIN? Where in the world did a little guy like you learn to be a lumberjack?" He quickly replied, "It was in the Sahara Forest, where I became one of the best there ever was." Suddenly, realizing it was time to become his straight man again, I said, "Sahara Forest? You mean the Sahara Desert, don't you?" He said, "YEAH NOW!"

Munch was at death's door for several months in the late seventies when a transplant and subsequent perfect kidney match saved his life and made him good as new. What a blessing those added years gave a lot of people, yours truly among them. With his health greatly improved, he wanted to progress in the Music Business that he loved so much and that meant moving on. He felt the best way was to hit the road with big name recording acts and experience the highest levels the entertainment field had to offer. He came to me one day and said, "Pops, I hate to leave you guys more than anything, but I got to go out there to see, feel and taste what the super big-time is all about." I gave him my blessing, and he left.

He didn't come around much due to his heavy road schedule with several top recording stars (at the time), including Barbara Mandrell and T.G. Sheppard. I rarely saw him during the next couple of years but somehow I always knew where he was. He continued to be in my heart and prayers until the end. I will always remember those special moments on stage at The Harmony House when he would walk up to my 6'4" frame wearing his solid white suit, shoes and scarf. He would then look up at me and point to the ceiling shouting loudly, "DI-PLANE, BOSS, DI-PLANE" (this was the opening line from the popular seventies TV Show Fantasy Island). When the uproarious laughter would finally die down, he and I would proceed to entertain the crowd with several old stage routines we had rehearsed. Audiences always seem to appreciate our performances and simply adored the "Little Guy in the White Suit."

"DI-PLANE, BOSS, DI-PLANE!"

Donnie 'Munchkin' Maloney, onstage with the Four
Guys at The Harmony House in Nashville.

Fast-forward to a regular Four Guy's stage show at The Stagedoor Lounge at The Opryland Hotel. This new venue became our home base from 1985 to 1989 after a ten-year run at The Harmony House. It was Thursday night, July 26, 1986. I was handed a business card from a guest who had traveled from Memphis to see our show that night. The guest said he had followed our group and individual members of our organization for many years. On the back of his business card, he had written, "WHERE'S THE MUNCHKIN?" I replied that I hadn't heard from Munch lately and then related what I knew of his whereabouts since leaving our group about four-years earlier. Ironically, about 30-minutes later that same night, a band member hurried into our dressing room and informed us that "The Munchkin" had been rushed to Vanderbilt Hospital in Nashville, in serious condition and was not expected to live through the night. He did live through the night and most of the next. But around 6:00 A.M. Saturday morning, July 28, 1986, Munch passed away. He had just celebrated his 30th birthday. Though it's been many years since his passing, a terrible chill of sadness just came over my body as I wrote the prior line.

Donnie "Munchkin" Maloney was his name. He was a Sound and Lightman. He was an Errand Runner, Chauffeur, Babysitter, Bus Driver, Concessionaire, Road Manager and Comedy Partner. He was a constant morale booster to all who knew him. He was virtually without an enemy in the world, a blessing most of us never receive. He was all these things and so much more. Most importantly to me, he was my very special friend and even now, I miss him deeply. He most assuredly will live in my heart and mind for as long as I live. He gave new meaning to the phrase, "YA GOTTA HAVE HEART," and HIS favorite, "I'M TELLIN' YOU WHAT'S THE TRUTH!"

CHAPTER THIRTY-FIVE
ALWAYS LEAVE 'EM
WANTING MORE...PLEASE

When a Club Owner, Show Promoter, TV or Radio Producer says he wants you to perform within the confines of a specific timeframe, by all means adhere strictly to his wishes. In fact, whenever possible, get off the stage early. Too many entertainers are unable to realize when it's time to make their exit and end up wearing out their welcome. Yes, many acts have a hard-core group of fans who could and would sit and listen for hours, but when you're performing to the masses, more often than not you are entertaining a diverse group of people who may certainly like what you do but do not necessarily want to hear you do it until the sun comes up.

I recall one night during an annual Fan Fair Celebration in Nashville. We (The Four Guys) were set to host the 11:30 P.M. portion (last show) of The Grand Ole Opry. For no specific reason, it had been a long, grueling day. We had spent countless hours signing autographs in our booth and in those of The Opry and The Ernest Tubb Record Shop. We also had performed on an Opry Matinee, the early Opry Show, and two shows at The Harmony House.

The late Johnny Russell was notorious for running over during the last Opry show whenever he would appear. He was scheduled to perform on the late show that night. I ran into Johnny in the hallway near the dressing rooms just prior to show-time. I later realized I made a huge mistake when I told him that we were all pretty tired and would appreciate everyone doing only their scheduled two songs so that we could end the show on time, midnight.

I must tell you here that The Four Guys in general (and me in particular) had been clowning around with the good Mr. Russell for more than twenty-five years, going back to our touring time together with The Charley Pride Show. To demonstrate a "chink" in our armor that we might be a little tired and wanted to go home on time was all he needed to hear. The show ran smoothly for the first 20-minutes with all the acts doing their songs and gracefully leaving the stage. I called Johnny out for his second and final tune, which he performed to a huge round of applause. Normally, there would be a final one-minute commercial with the Opry announcer, throwing it back to me for closing "thank yous" and one last song by the host act, in this case, The Four Guys. However, Johnny had decided before the show began that this is where he would mess with us/me like we had never been messed with before.

Instead of leaving the stage after his final song, he walked over to the Staff Announcer's podium and began helping him read the final commercial. The announcer, Hairl Hensley, would read a commercial line and Johnny would interrupt, comment on the line and adlib a humorous twist to it. Nearly ten-minutes passed with Russell kibitzing with Hensley and generally interfering with the job he (Hensley) was trying to perform.

When the commercial was finally over, Johnny proceeded to make a transition into a totally different comedy routine, all the while standing at the announcer's podium and using HIS mike. With the audience listening to Johnny, they were also watching me to see just how I was going to handle the moment. The audience was keenly aware that this hugely popular Opry entertainer had completely taken over a show being hosted by The Four Guys. I began using not so subtle gestures directed at Russell, such as pointing to my watch and acting like I was falling asleep. If there had been a box of corn flakes handy, I would have walked to the podium and placed it in front of John (signifying breakfast time was drawing near).

When I finally looked at the stage clock, it read 12:20 A.M. The show had gone over twenty-minutes and Russell was still talking. I knew something had to happen fast. Suddenly, I grabbed the closest mike and in a loud, high-pitched ringmaster tone of voice, I interrupted Johnny and said, "LADIES and GENTLEMEN, SAY GOODNIGHT TO MR. JOHNNY RUSSELL." Then, remembering a line from an old MARTIN and LEWIS skit, I added, "JOHNNY, BE SURE TO SWEEP UP THE BUILDING, TURN OUT THE LIGHTS and LOCK UP. THE REST OF US ARE GOING HOME." With that, I signaled the curtain guy to bring it down fast. He did, and we all had a big laugh.

The audience never heard the funniest remark of the evening. It came from the Opry's Sound Director, Conrad Jones, shortly after the curtain was lowered. He casually told Lighting Director, Suzie Ray that I was not necessarily his favorite Four Guy; but that he thought he WOULD send me a 12-pack of beer the very next Christmas.

If I continue to ramble on with more "Show-Biz" stories and advice for the future of your career, I will not be taking my own advice seriously and will not leave you wanting more, assuming you wanted any of this to begin with.

In closing, I sincerely hope that you have found many words of wisdom in the preceding chapters and that they help you greatly in your efforts to reach the top of the entertainment world.

Remember, there's much more to our business than just having hit records, though that is certainly where you should place your initial focus. Many Country Music acts have found new life in Radio, TV, The Movies and The Theatre after their recording careers began to fade. It's a big business and with the right stuff, you can find a place in it.

One final thought: AS YOU GO DOWN LIFE'S LONG, LONESOME SHOW-BIZ HIGHWAY, THEY SAY OPPORTUNITY KNOCKS BUT ONCE. BUT REMEMBER, REGULAR UNLEADED KNOCKS TIME AND TIME AGAIN! (Wellington, I can't believe you closed your first book with that hokey, line). HOSS, SWEEP UP THE BUILDING, TURN OUT THE LIGHTS and LOCK UP...THE REST OF US ARE GOING HOME!

Meanwhile, to those of you WHO WANT TO BECOME A COUNTRY MUSIC STAR...GOOD LUCK, HAVE FUN AND ENJOY THE RIDE!

Printed in the United States
46573LVS00008B/52-72

9 781420 805789